Knitter's at HOME

photography by
Alexis Xenakis

B

Knitter's at HOME

a publication of XRX Books

PUBLISHER
Alexis Yiorgos Xenakis

COEDITORS
Rick Mondragon
Elaine Rowley

MANAGING EDITOR
Karen Bright

PROJECT COORDINATOR
Sue Kay Nelson

EDITORIAL COORDINATOR
Elisabeth Robinson

INSTRUCTION EDITOR
Joni Coniglio

INSTRUCTION ASSISTANTS
Kirsten Coniglio
Kelly Rokke
Carol Thompson

GRAPHIC DESIGNER
Natalie Sorenson

PHOTOGRAPHER
Alexis Yiorgos Xenakis

STYLIST
Rick Mondragon

PHOTO ASSISTANT
Lisa Mannes

CHIEF EXECUTIVE OFFICER
Benjamin Levisay

DIRECTOR, PUBLISHING SERVICES
David Xenakis

TECHNICAL ILLUSTRATOR
Carol Skallerud

PRODUCTION DIRECTOR & COLOR SPECIALIST
Dennis Pearson

BOOK PRODUCTION MANAGER
Greg Hoogeveen

DIGITAL PREPRESS
Everett Baker

MARKETING MANAGER
Lisa Mannes

BOOKS DISTRIBUTION
Mavis Smith

MIS
Jason Bittner

FIRST PUBLISHED IN THE USA IN 2009 BY XRX, INC.

ISBN 13: 9781933064147
Produced in Sioux Falls, South Dakota, by XRX, Inc.,
PO Box 965
Sioux Falls, SD
57101-0965
USA
605.338.2450

Contents

Americana

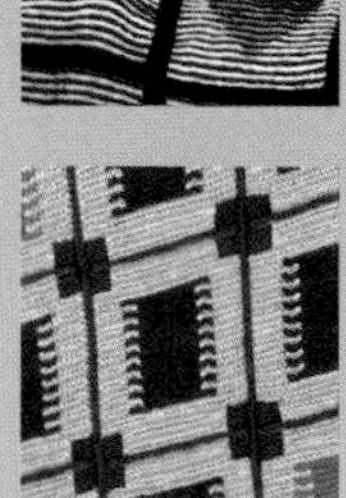

Colors of the World

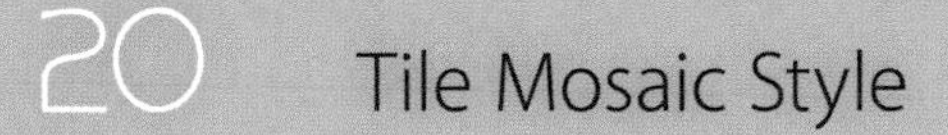

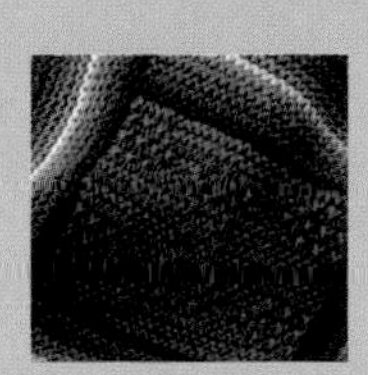

Textures at Home

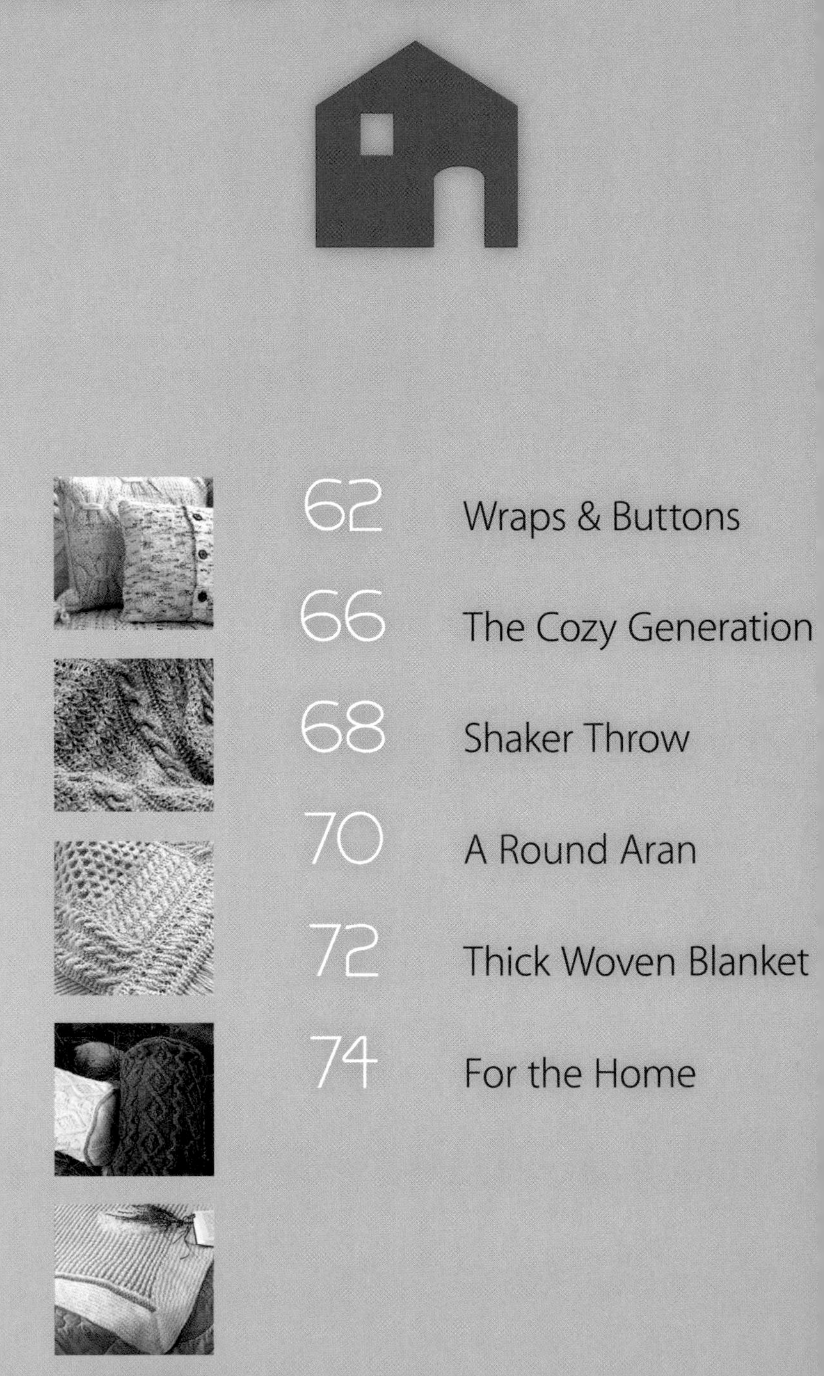

Soft Geometry

Welcome home

Home is where our days begin and end.

Home is where we dream our dreams, pursue our passions, and plan our projects.

Home is where we create beauty, warmth, and comfort — one stitch at a time.

Knits make it home.

Americana

1-color Chart

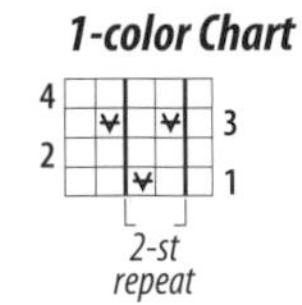

2-color Chart

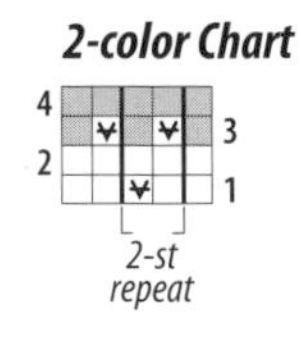

Stitch key

☐ *Knit on RS, purl on WS*

☒ *Sl 1 purlwise with yarn in front*

Color key (2-color Chart)

☐ *MC*

▩ *CC*

American Spirit

Designed by
Laura Polley

EASY +

Approximately 48" × 62½"

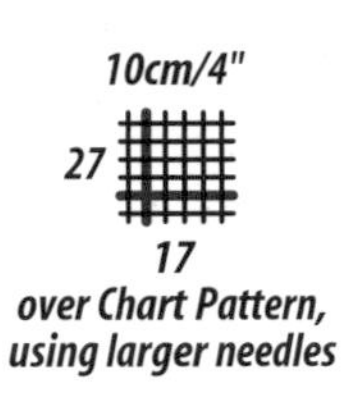

over Chart Pattern, using larger needles

Medium weight
A • 1235 yds
B • 760 yds
C • 545 yds

6mm/US 10, or size to obtain gauge

5mm/US 8, 74cm/29" long or longer

BROWN SHEEP Lamb's Pride Worsted (85% wool, 15% mohair; 4oz/113g; 190yd/173m) in M10 Crème (A), M83 Raspberry (B), M82 Blue Flannel (C)

Notes

1 Afghan consists of 13 strips that are knit separately and sewn together. **2** Work each strip in 1-color or 2-color Chart patterns, following strip diagrams for colors.

Strip 1 *(Make 7)*

With larger needles and A, cast on 17 stitches. Work in 1-color Chart pattern for 24 rows, then work 2-color Chart pattern, using A as MC and B as CC, for 24 rows. Continue working in 1-color and 2-color Chart patterns, following strip diagram for colors of each 24-row block. Bind off with A after last block.

Strip 2 *(Make 4)*

With larger needles and B, cast on 17 stitches. Work in 2-color Chart pattern, using B as MC and A as CC, for 24 rows, then with B, work 1-color Chart for 24 rows. Continue working in 1-color and 2-color Chart patterns, following strip diagram for colors of each 24-row block. Bind off with A after last block.

Strip 3 *(Make 2)*

With larger needles and C, cast on 17 stitches. Work in 2-color Chart pattern, using C as MC and A as CC, for 24 rows, then work 2-color Chart pattern, using C as MC and B as CC, for 24 rows. Continue working 1-color and 2-color Chart patterns, following strip diagram for colors of each 24-row block. Bind off with A after last block.

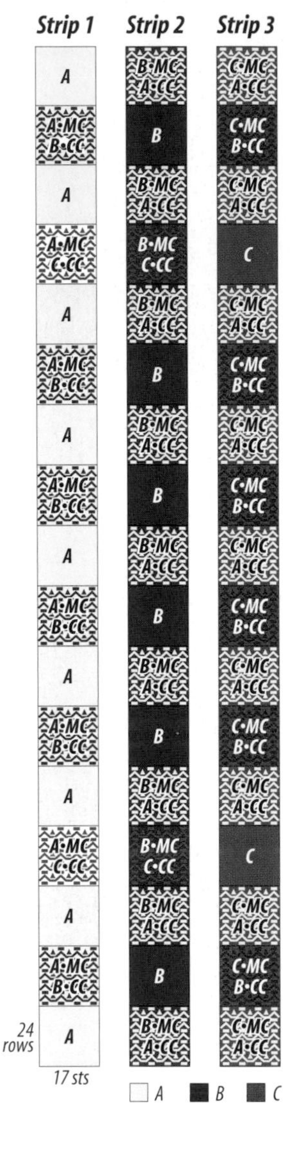

Finishing

Block strips and sew them together, following joining diagram, and making sure blocks align.

Side borders

With RS facing, smaller needles, and C, pick up and knit 289 stitches along side edge (17 stitches per block). Knit 7 rows. Bind off purlwise on RS. Repeat for other side.

Upper and lower borders

Work as for side borders, picking up 15 stitches along each block, and 5 stitches along side borders—205 stitches.

Joining strips

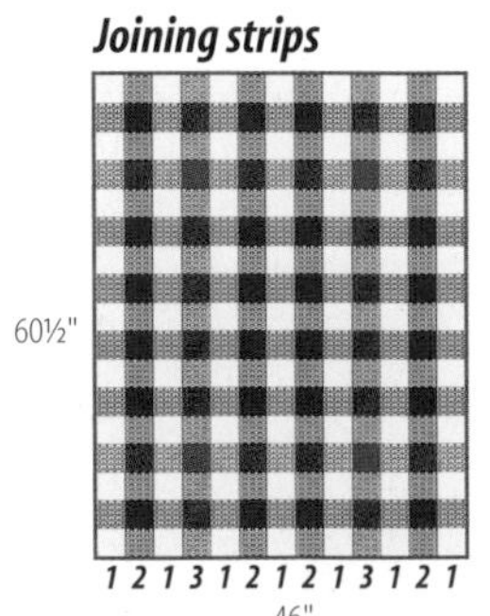

Whirligigs

Designed by
Barbara Venishnick

INTERMEDIATE

43" × 71" blocked

10cm/4"

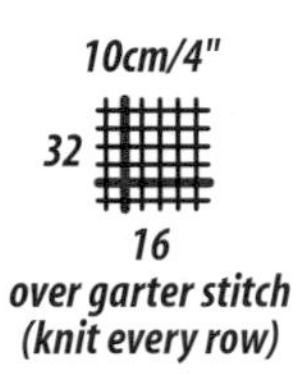

32

16
over garter stitch (knit every row)

Medium weight
MC • 1525 yds
CC1 • 980 yds
CC2 • 220 yds

5mm/US 8, or size to obtain gauge

3.75mm/F

REYNOLDS Lite-Lopi
(100% wool; 1¾oz/50g; 109yd/100m)
in 0051 White (MC), 0434 Red (CC1),
0442 Blue (CC2)

Notes

1 See *School*, page 102, for intarsia, single crochet (sc), double crochet (dc), and chain (ch) stitch. **2** At color changes, bring new color under old on WS of work to prevent holes. **3** Use separate length of yarn for each color area on rows 11–38 and rows 25–38.

Chart A square *(Make 32)*

Cast on 14 stitches with MC, then 14 stitches with CC1. Work 48 rows of Chart A. Bind off, matching colors.

Chart B square *(Make 28)*

Work as for Chart A square, working 48 rows of Chart B.

Finishing

Block squares to measurements. Join squares as follows: Sew A squares together in 8 units of 4 squares each, then sew B squares around A squares, following Joining Diagram for placement.

Crocheted edging

Round 1 With RS facing, crochet hook and CC2, begin at lower right corner and work as follows: * work 7 sc, skip 1 stitch, work 4 dc in next stitch, skip 1 stitch; repeat from * around entire edge of afghan, working into knit rows between garter ridges when working along a side edge of a square, and working 4 dc at corners, regardless of where it falls in the sequence. ***Round 2*** With MC, work 1 sc in each stitch of previous round, working 2 sc in each of the 4 dc at corners.

Ties (Make 23)

With crochet hook and CC2, ch 48. Weave ends into chain. With crochet hook, draw one end of chain-tie down through block approximately ¼" from center point of pinwheel motif (joining point of 4 squares), then up again approximately ¼" on other side of center point. Tie ends into a bow.

Chart A

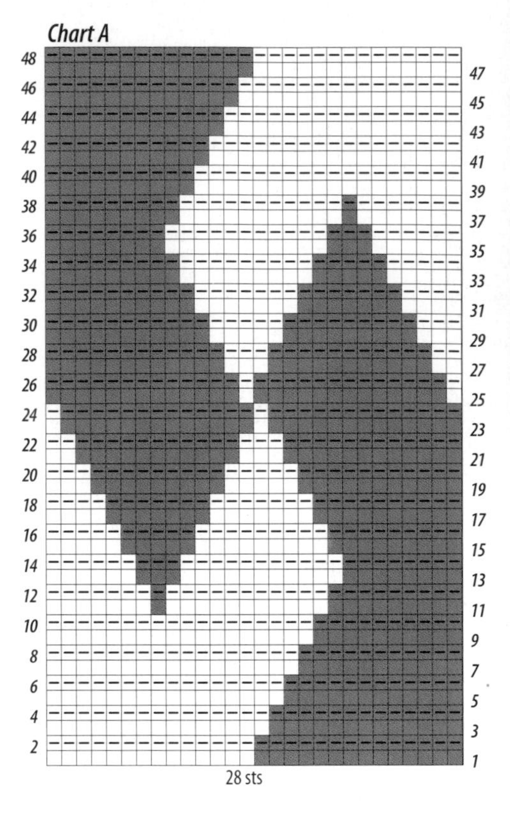

Chart B

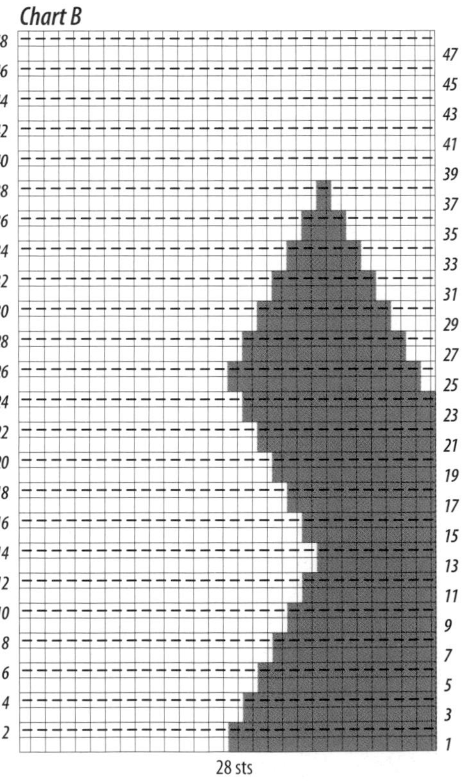

Color key

Stitch key

□ *Knit on RS*
⊟ *Knit on WS*

Joining Diagram
Join A squares in groups of 4.
Join eight 4-square units of Chart A.
7"
7"
Border with B squares.
Try your own colors online at
www.KnittingUniverse.com/PAINTBOX.

EASY+

14" × 14"

Medium (Bulky, Super bulky) weight

10cm/4"

24 (17, 12)

20 (13, 10)
over stockinette stitch (knit on RS, purl on WS)

Medium weight
A, B & C • 197 yds each

Bulky weight
A, B & C • 153 yds each

Super bulky
A, B & C • 108 yds each

4mm/US 6, 6mm/US10, 10mm/US15, or size to obtain gauge

&

14" square pillow form for each pillow

LION BRAND Wool Ease Worsted weight (80% acrylic, 20% wool; 3oz/85g; 197yd/180m) 138 Cranberry (A), 114 Denim (B), 099 Fisherman (C);

Chunky weight (80% acrylic, 20% wool; 5oz/140g; 153yd/140m) 139 Huckleberry (A), 115 Bay Harbor (B), 099 Fisherman (C);

Thick and Quick (80% acrylic, 20% wool; 6oz/170g; 108yd/98m) 138 Cranberry (A), 114 Denim (B), 099 Fisherman (C)

Americana Cushions

Designed by
Knitter's Design Team

Notes

1 See *School*, page 102, for intarsia. **2** When working horizontal stripes, carry yarns along side of work. **3** When working intarsia (vertical) stripes, use separate lengths of yarn for each color. Bring new color under old color to twist yarns and prevent holes. **4** Instructions are given for Medium (Bulky, Super bulky) weight pillows.

Front

With A, cast on 72 (50, 37) stitches. Work Chart B, for 84 (60, 42) rows. Bind off.

Back

Medium weight pillow (right)

With A, cast on 72 stitches. Work Chart A for 84 rows. Bind off.

Bulky weight pillow (center)

Cast on 50 stitches as follows: 11 stitches A, 6 stitches C, 10 stitches B, 6 stitches A, 10 stitches C, 7 stitches A. Beginning with a knit row, work in stockinette stitch in colors as established until piece measures same length as front. Bind off.

Super bulky weight pillow (left)

Cast on 37 stitches as follows: 6 stitches A, 5 stitches B, 10 stitches C, 5 stitches A, 11 stitches B. Beginning with a knit row, work in stockinette stitch in colors as established until piece measures same length as front. Bind off.

Finishing

Block pieces. Sew front to back, leaving one side open. Insert pillow form and sew remaining seam.

Chart A

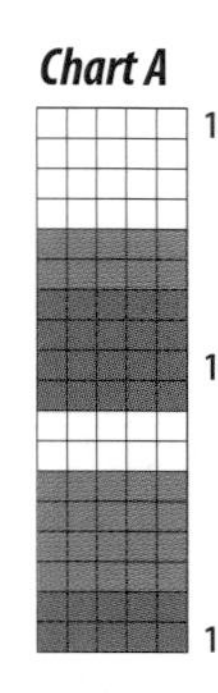

Chart B

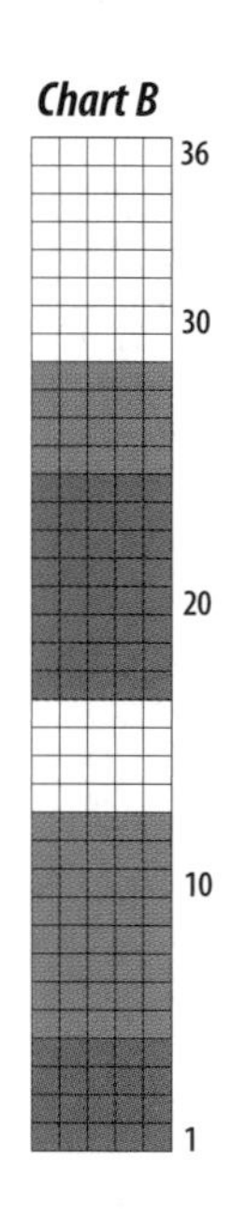

Stitch key

Color key

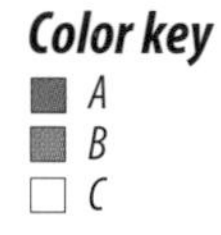

Try your own colors online at
www.KnittingUniverse.com/PAINTBOX.

Knit & Purl Pillow

Designer
Jill Wolcott

EASY+

16" × 16"

10cm/4"

40

20

over Linen Stitch using MC, washed, dried flat, and steamed

1 2 3 **4** 5 6

Medium weight

MC • 440 yards for one pillow

Knit chart • 24 yds coral, 16 yds each honey gold, peach, celadon
Purl chart • 24 yds celadon, 16 yds rose, 8 yds honey gold
Fringe • 80 yds assorted colors

4.5mm/US 7, or size to obtain gauge

• 16" square pillow form
• tapestry needle for embroidery

REYNOLDS Paterna (100% wool; 1¾oz/50g; 110yd/100m) 24 Ecru (MC); Paternayan Persian Wool (100% wool; 8yd/7.4m) 952 Coral, 731 Honey Gold, 846 Peach, 538 Celadon, 931 Rose

Linen Stitch *(Over an even number of stitches)*

Row 1 (RS) K1, *slip 1 purlwise with yarn in front, k1; repeat from * to last stitch, k1.
Row 2 P1, *slip 1 purlwise with yarn in back, p1; repeat from * to last stitch, p1. Repeat rows 1–2 for Linen Stitch.

Back/Front

With MC, cast on 82 stitches. Work 160 rows in Linen Stitch. Piece measures approximately 16" from beginning. Bind off.

Finishing

Block pieces. Mark horizontal and vertical center lines of pieces with basting thread. Work cross-stitch, following either Knit or Purl chart as follows: separate lengths of Persian wool into 3 strands; thread 2 strands in needle for embroidery. Follow charts from top to bottom, using center lines as reference. After embroidery, steam pieces and allow to dry completely. Complete as shown on page 12.

CROSS-STITCH EMBROIDERY

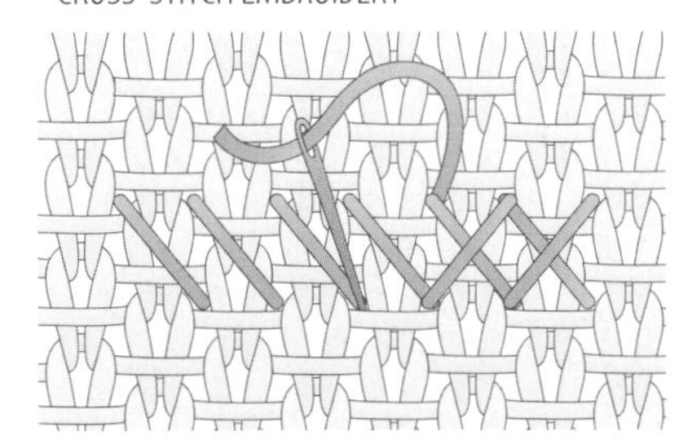

Chart notes

1 Selvage stitches do not appear on cross-stitch charts.

2 Each square of the cross-stitch chart is 1 knitted stitch wide and 1 slip stitch (2 rows) high.

Color key

- *Rose*
- *Coral*
- *Honey gold*
- *Peach*
- *Celadon*

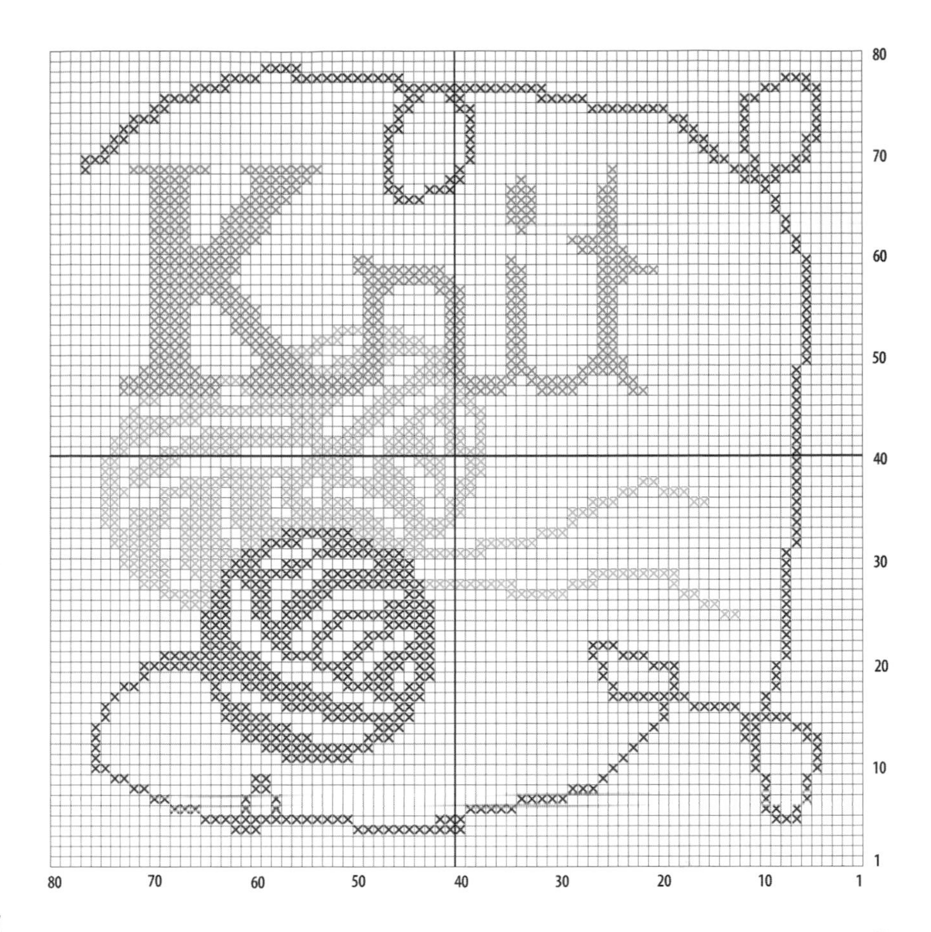

Fringe

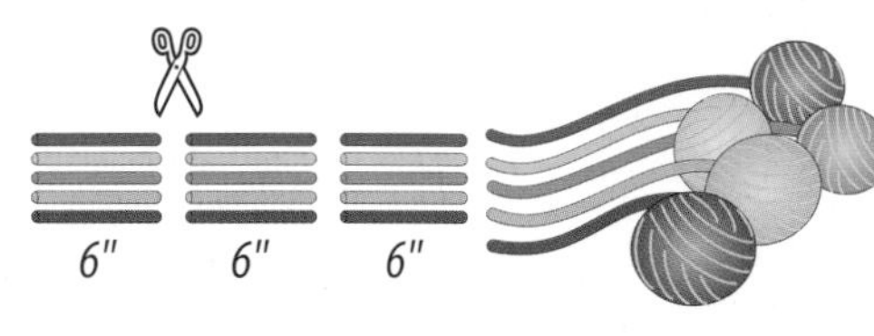

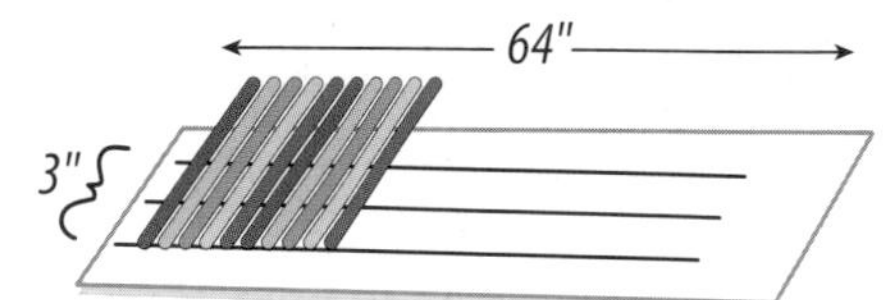

1 Cut 6" lengths of Persian wool (unseparated). On tissue or paper, draw 3 lines, each 64" long and 1½" apart from each other. Lay lengths of wool so that one end touches one of the outside lines, crossing the other two. Wool should be dense without bunching.

2 Machine stitch down center line. Fold yarn back over stitching so that other end lies on top of first end. Stitch again. Remove paper.

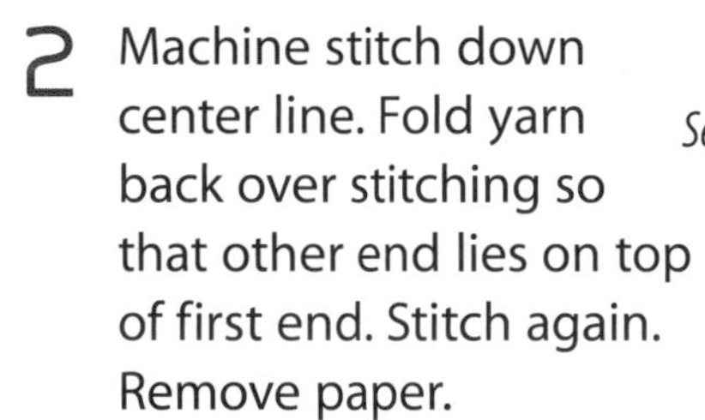

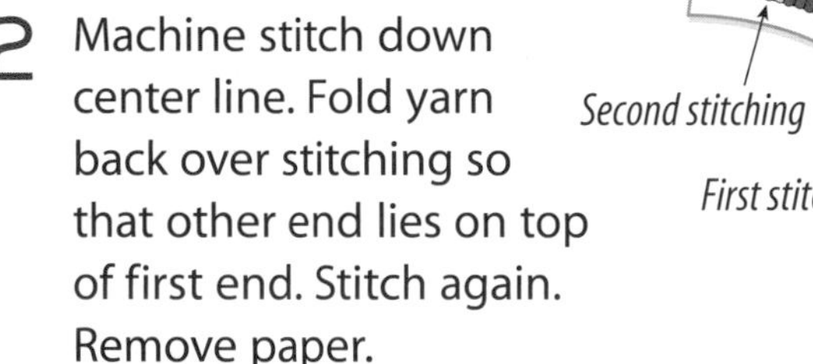

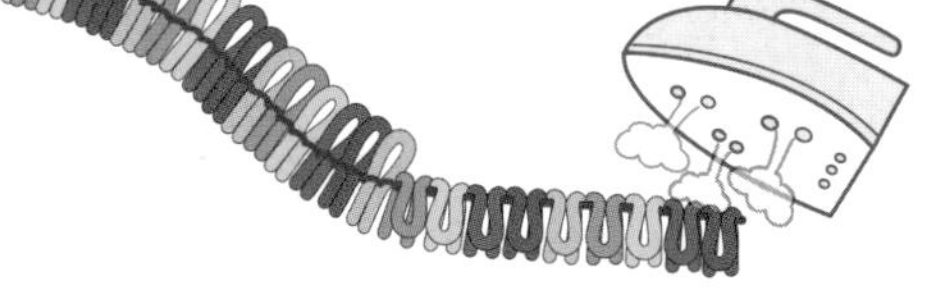

3 Fold fringe along stitching line and steam.

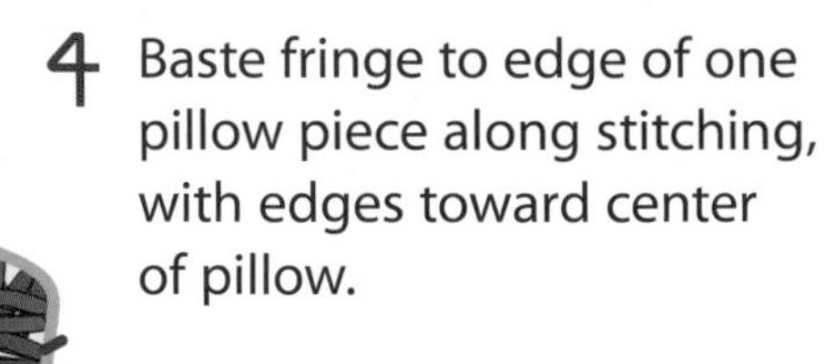

4 Baste fringe to edge of one pillow piece along stitching, with edges toward center of pillow.

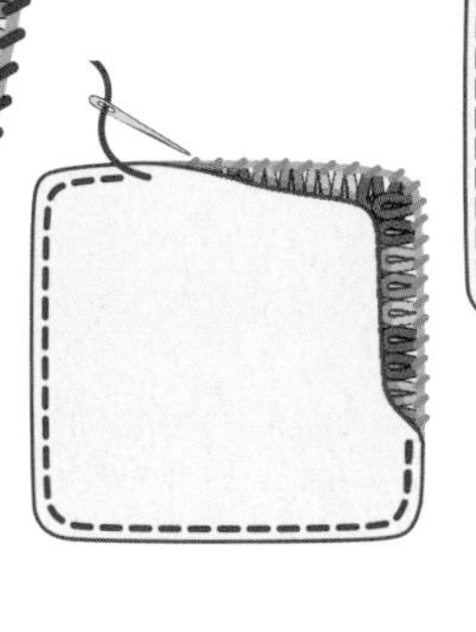

5 With RS together, backstitch pillow pieces together, stitching through fringe along 3 sides and for 3–4" in from each corner on 4th side.

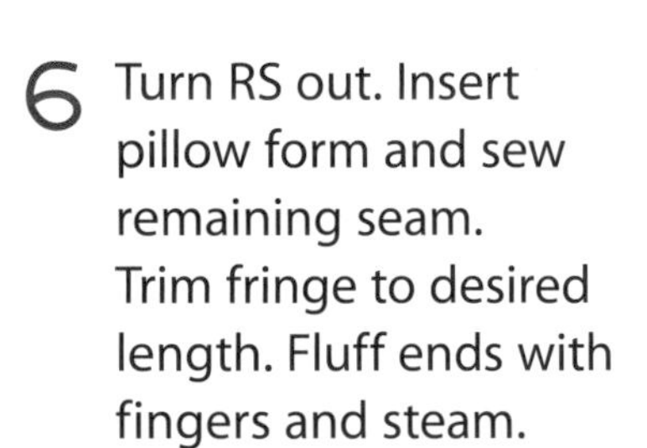

6 Turn RS out. Insert pillow form and sew remaining seam. Trim fringe to desired length. Fluff ends with fingers and steam.

Next page, Stars and Hearts at instructions follow.

Stars and Hearts

Designed by
Gerdine Crawford-Strong

INTERMEDIATE

48½" × 52¾"
after blocking

10cm/4"

30

16
over garter stitch (knit every row)

1 2 3 4 **5** 6

Bulky weight
A & B • 810 yds each
C • 675 yds

5.5mm/US 9, or size to obtain gauge

&

tapestry needle

ORIGINAL YARN

MANOS DEL URUGUAY 100% Wool (100% wool; 3½oz/100g; 135yd/123m) in 14 White (A), 48 Red (B), 11 Navy (C)

Notes

1 See *School*, page 102, for intarsia. **2** Bring new color under old at color change to prevent holes. **3** Cast on all stitches using C. **4** Work stitches at each side of 41-stitch block pattern of each square in garter stitch with separate balls of C.

Center Strips

6 Center Squares (Make 2 stars, 2 hearts, 2 stripes)
Cast on 47 stitches. Knit **4** rows (2 garter ridges on RS). ***Begin Block Pattern: Row 1*** (RS) Knit 3C, work 41 stitches of block pattern, knit 3C. ***Row 2*** Knit 3C, work 41 stitches of block pattern, knit 3C. Work through row 70 of block pattern. With one ball of C knit **4** rows. Bind off.

2 Upper Squares (Make 1 stripe, 1 heart)
Work as Center Square ***EXCEPT*** end with **8** rows (4 ridges) of C instead of 4.

2 Lower Squares (Make 1 star, 1 stripe)
Work as Center Square ***EXCEPT*** begin with **8** rows (4 ridges) of C instead of 4.

Left Strip

3 Center Squares (Make 1 heart, 1 stripe, 1 star)
Cast on 50 stitches. Knit **4** rows. ***Begin Block Pattern: Row 1*** (RS) Knit 3C, work 41 stitches of block pattern, knit 6C. ***Row 2*** Knit 6C, work 41 stitches of block pattern, knit 3C. Work through row 70 of block pattern. With one ball of C knit **4** rows. Bind off.

1 Upper Corner Square (Make 1 star)
Work as Center-Left square ***EXCEPT*** end with **8** rows (4 ridges) of C instead of 4.

1 Lower Corner Square (Make 1 heart)
Work as Center-Left square ***EXCEPT*** begin with **8** rows (4 ridges) of C instead of 4.

Right Strip

3 Center Squares (Make 1 heart, 1 stripe, 1 star)
Cast on 50 stitches. Knit **4** rows. ***Begin Block Pattern: Row 1*** (RS) Knit 6C, work 41 stitches of block pattern, knit 3C. ***Row 2*** Knit 3C, work 41 stitches of block pattern, knit 6C. Work through row 70 of block pattern. With one ball of C knit **4** rows. Bind off.

1 Upper Corner Square (Make 1 star)
Work as Center-Right square ***EXCEPT*** end with **8** rows (4 ridges) of C instead of 4.

1 Lower Corner Square (Make 1 heart)
Work as Center-Right square ***EXCEPT*** begin with **8** rows (4 ridges) of C instead of 4.

Finishing

Block squares to measurements. With C, sew squares together, following Joining Diagram.

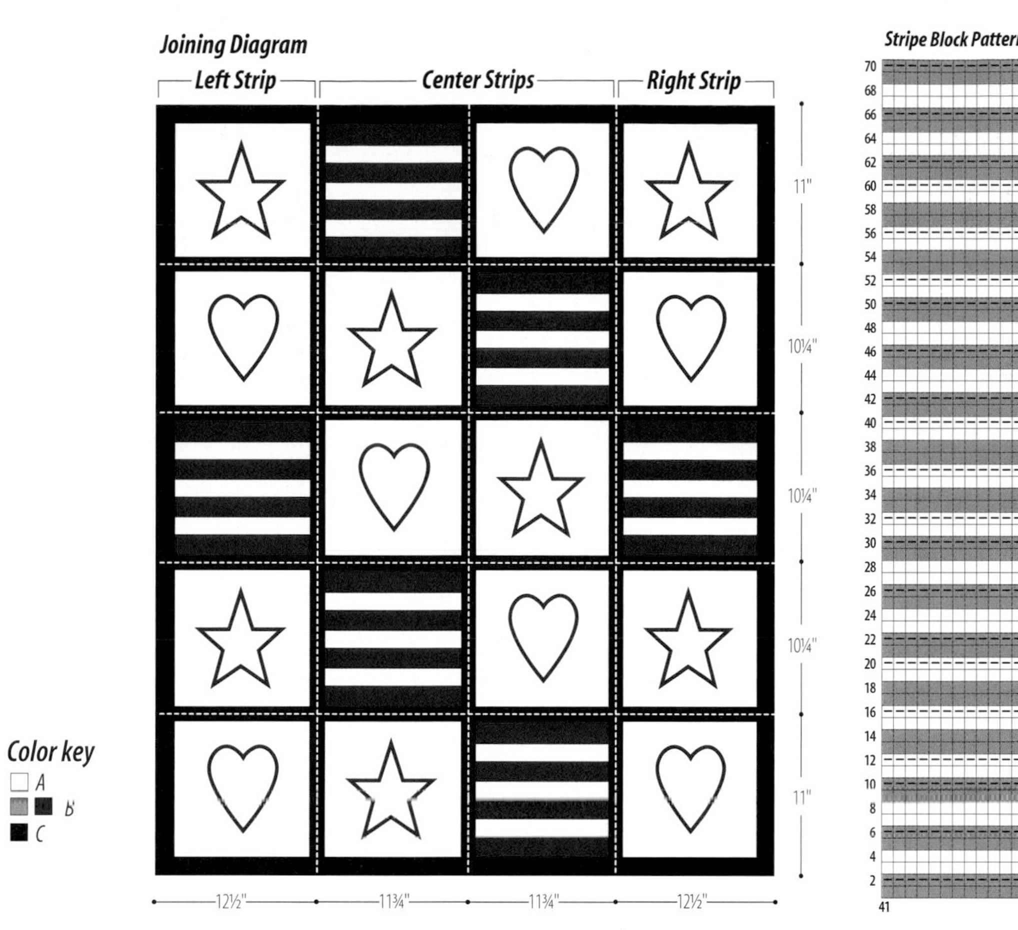

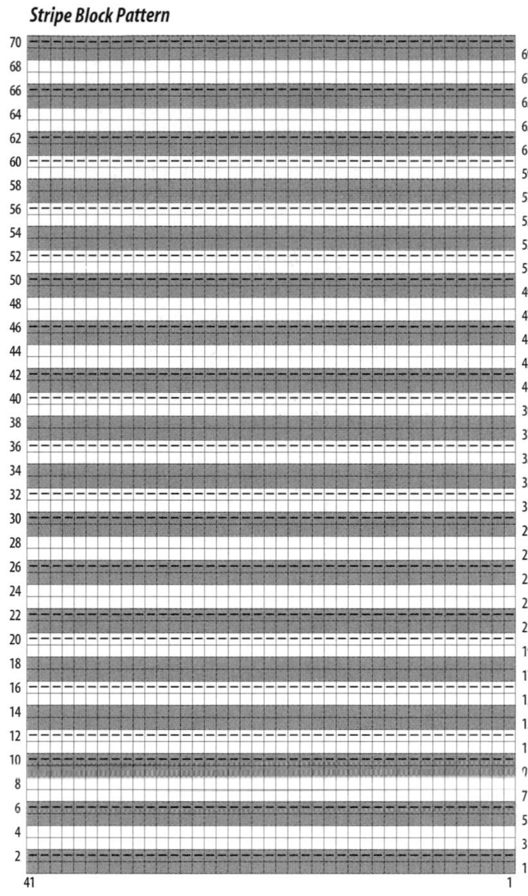

Stitch key

- Knit on RS, purl on WS
- Knit on WS

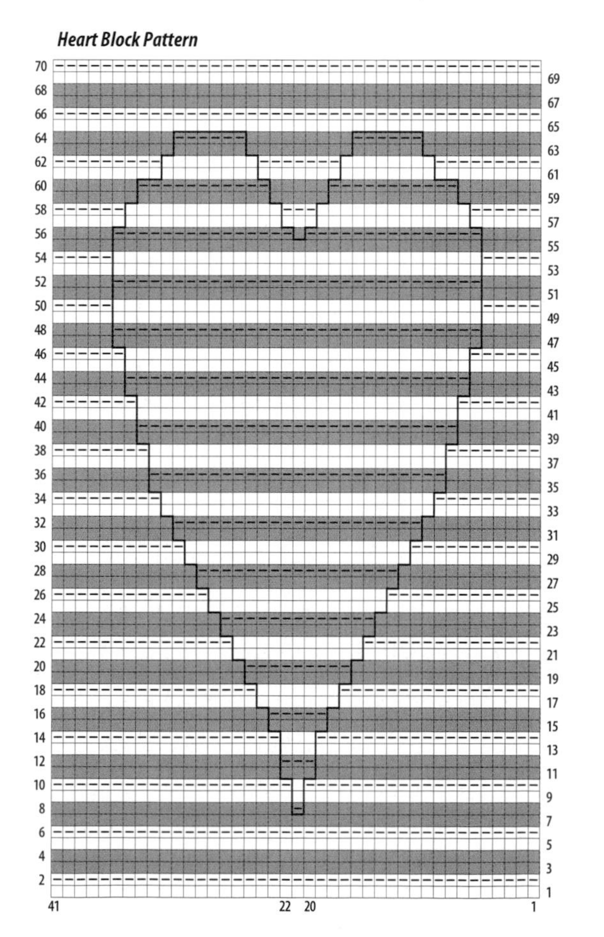

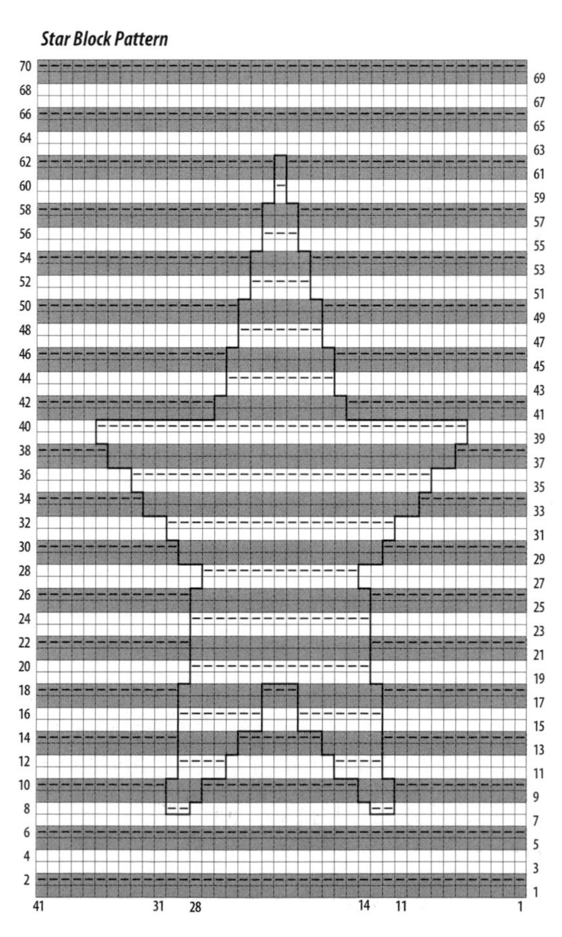

Drunken Squares

Designed by
Barbara Venishnick

INTERMEDIATE +

42" × 49"

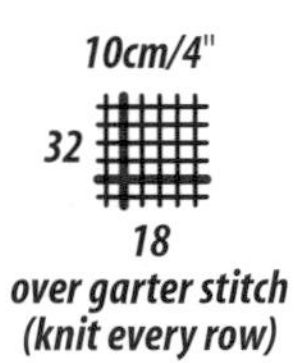

over garter stitch (knit every row)

Medium weight
A • 820 yds
B • 855 yds
C, E, F • 210 yds each
D • 340 yds
G • 220 yds

4mm/US 6, or size to obtain gauge

4mm/G

tapestry needle

CASCADE YARNS Cascade 220 (100% wool; 3½oz/100g; 220yd/200m) in 4011 Sparrow (A), 8407 Oyster (B), 9404 Ruby (C), 9408 Cordovan (D), 4001 Bluestone (E), 4005 Sea (F), 9411 Rain Forest (G) 0434 Red (CC1), 0442 Blue (CC2)

Notes

1 See *School*, page 102, for long-tail cast-on, intarsia, chain stitch embroidery, and single crochet (sc). **2** Twist yarns together on WS at color changes to prevent holes. **3** Use 4 separate lengths of C for each square; use separate lengths of A and B on each side of center motif on chart rows 12–17. **4** When a color must be carried over 3 or 4 stitches (color A on chart row 8 for example) move yarn into position on preceding row by catching it once under working yarn (on WS of work).

Square *(Make 21 squares using D for center motif, 11 using E, and 10 using F.)*

Using long-tail cast-on, cast on 32 stitches as follows: 5 stitches C, 22 stitches A, 5 stitches C. ***Work Square Chart*** Beginning with a WS row, work chart rows 1–11, then work rows 12–15 (using D, E, or F for center motif) 8 times, work through chart row 29. Bind off.

Finishing

Block squares. Join squares, using overcast seams, into columns following Joining Diagram for placement. Then join columns together. With crochet hook and G, work chain stitch embroidery between squares, working first horizontally, then vertically. With crochet hook and G, work 1 round sc evenly around edges, working 1 sc in each stitch, and 2 sc in each corner.

Joining Diagram

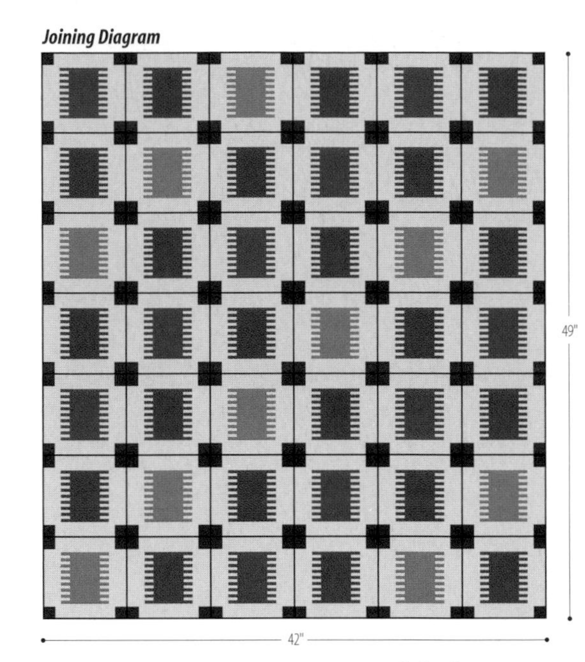

Square Chart

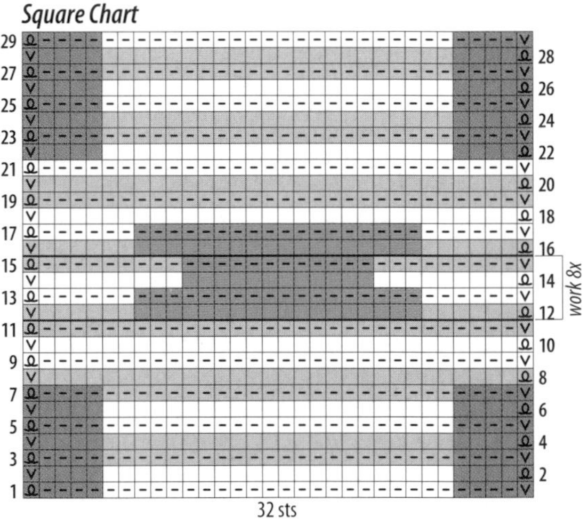

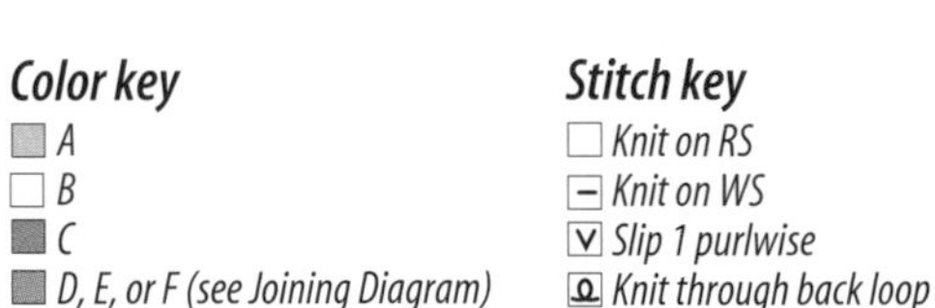

Try your own colors online at
www.KnittingUniverse.com/PAINTBOX.

Colors of the World

Tile Mosaic Style

Designed by
Ann Regis

INTERMEDIATE

Approximately 41½" × 54"

10cm/4"

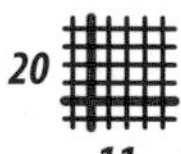

20

11

over garter stitch (knit every row) using 2 strands of yarn held together

1 2 3 4 5 6

• Light weight

A, B, C, & F • 270 yds each
D, E, & H • 540 yds each
G • 810 yds

9mm/US 13, or size to obtain gauge

9mm/US 13, 80cm/29" long or longer

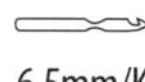

6.5mm/K

tapestry needle

FILATURA DI CROSA No. 501 (superwash wool; 1¾oz/50g; 136yd/123m) Teal (A), Purple (B), Brick (C), Navy (D), Burgundy (E), Forest green (F), Yellow (G); Zara (wool; 1¾oz/50g; 136yd/123m) Gold (H)

Notes

1 See *School*, page 102, for single crochet (sc), backward sc and slip-stitch (sl st) crochet.
2 Use 2 strands of yarn held together throughout.

Stripe Pattern

Knit 2 rows each in the following color sequence: D, E, F, B, H, G, H, B, F, E, D (22 rows).

Panel I (Make 2)

With D, cast on 29 stitches. Knit 1 row (first 2 rows of Stripe Pattern complete). Beginning with E, work 20 rows more in Stripe Pattern.
Work 38 rows of Chart A, using A for MC and C for CC. Work 22 rows of Stripe Pattern.
Work 38 rows of Chart A, using C for MC and A for CC. Work 22 rows of Stripe Pattern.
Work 38 rows of Chart A, using A for MC and C for CC. Work 22 rows of Stripe Pattern.
With D, bind off.

Panel II (Make 2)

With D, cast on 15 stitches. Knit 1 row (first 2 rows of Stripe Pattern complete). Beginning with E, work 20 rows more in Stripe Pattern.
Work 38 rows of Chart B, using B for MC and H for CC. Work 22 rows of Stripe Pattern.
Work 38 rows of Chart B, using H for MC and B for CC. Work 22 rows of Stripe Pattern.
Work 38 rows of Chart B, using B for MC and H for CC. Work 22 rows of Stripe Pattern.
With D, bind off.

Panel III (Make 1)

With D, cast on 29 stitches. Knit 1 row (first 2 rows of Stripe Pattern complete). Beginning with E, work 20 rows more in Stripe Pattern.
Work 38 rows of Chart A, using C for MC and A for CC. Work 22 rows of Stripe Pattern.
Work 38 rows of Chart C, using A for MC and C for CC. Work 22 rows of Stripe Pattern.
Work 38 rows of Chart A, using C for MC and A for CC. Work 22 rows of Stripe Pattern.
With D, bind off.

Chart A

29 sts

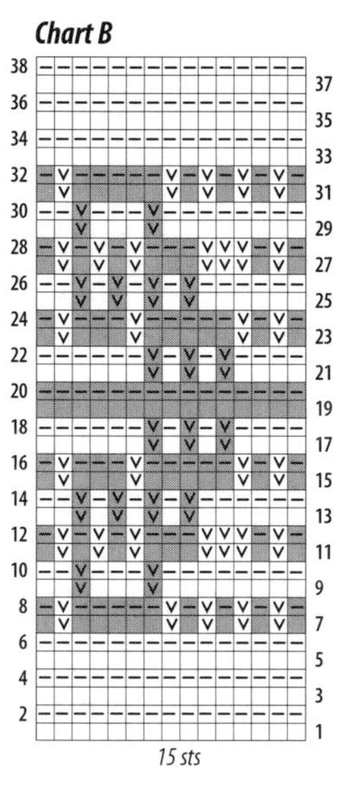

Stitch key

☐ *Knit on RS*
⊟ *Knit on WS*
☑ *Slip 1 purlwise with yarn at WS of work*

Color key

☐ *MC*
■ *CC*

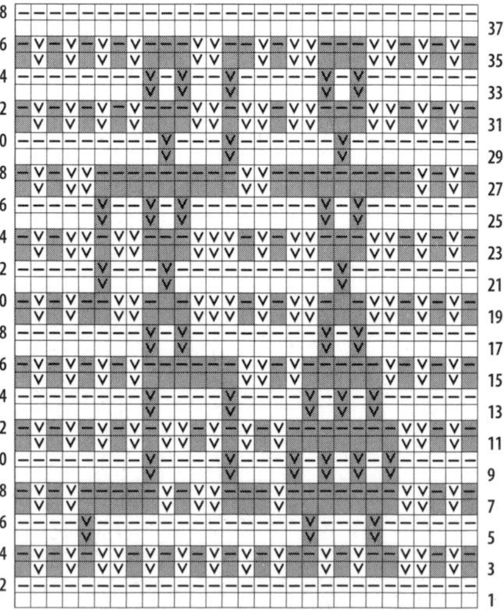

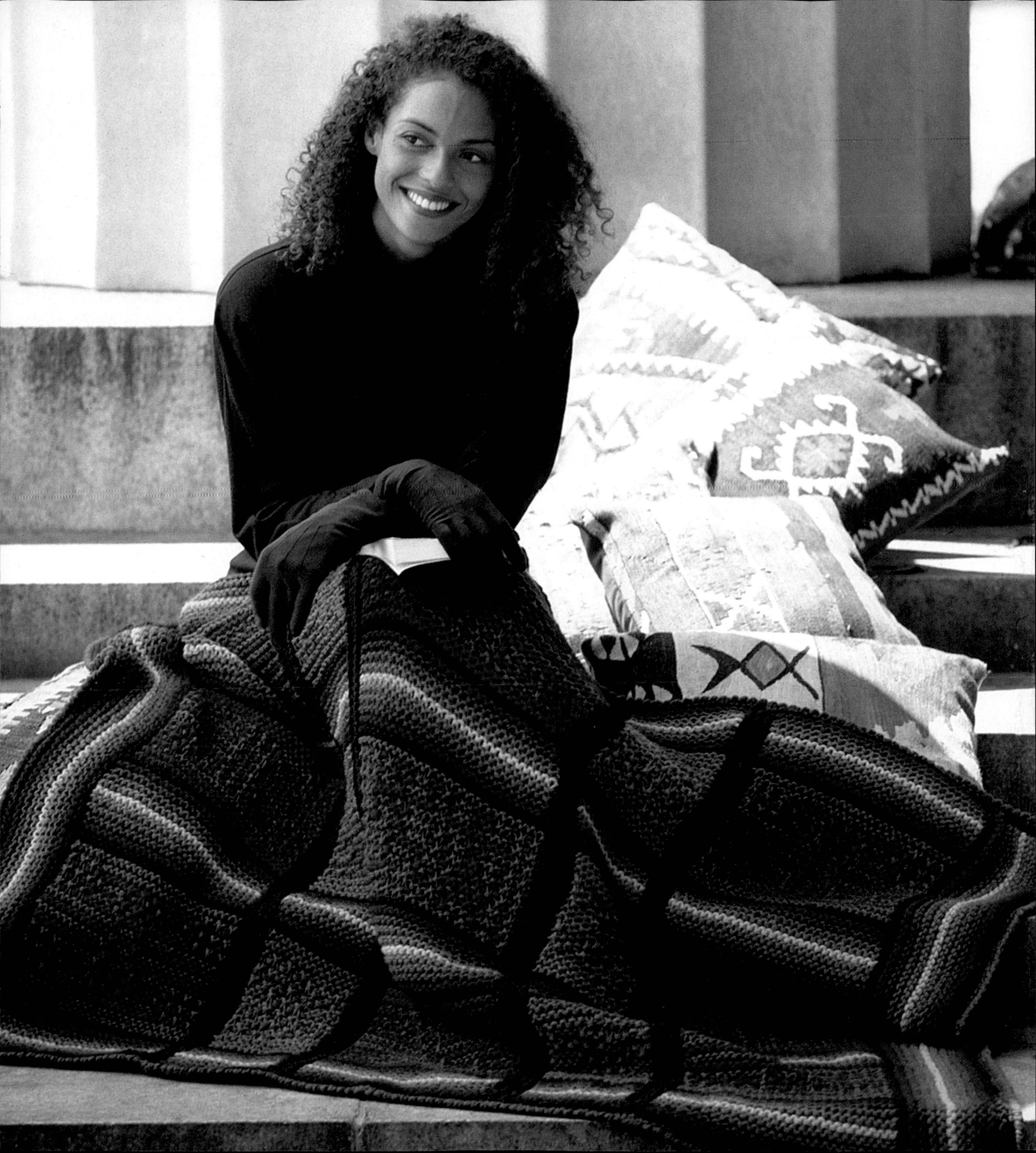

Finishing

Block pieces.

Side edging of panels

Work edging along long edges of each panel as follows: With RS facing, circular needle and D, pick up and knit 1 stitch for each garter ridge along long edge. Knit 1 row. Bind off loosely. With D, sew panels together as shown in Joining Diagram.

Side edging of afghan

With RS facing, circular needle and D, pick up and knit 1 stitch in each bound-off stitch along one side edge of afghan. Knit 1 row (first 2 rows of Stripe Pattern complete). Beginning with E, work 20 rows more in Stripe Pattern. Bind off loosely. Repeat along second side.

Crochet edging

With RS facing, crochet hook and A, begin at a corner and work 1 round sc evenly around entire edge of afghan, working 3 sc into each corner stitch. Join last stitch to first with sl st. Do not turn. Work 1 round backward sc. Join last stitch to first with sl st. Fasten off.

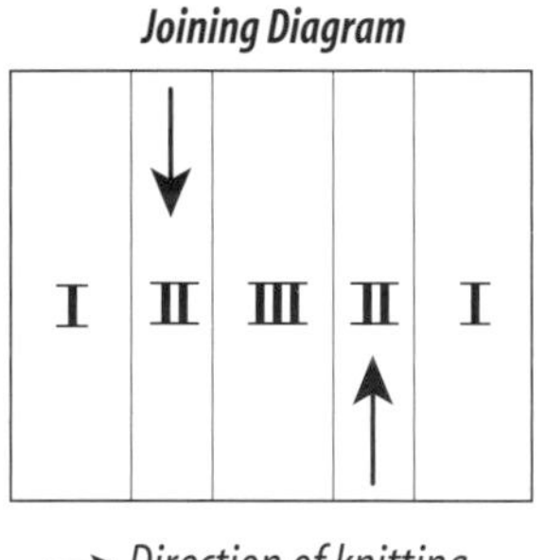

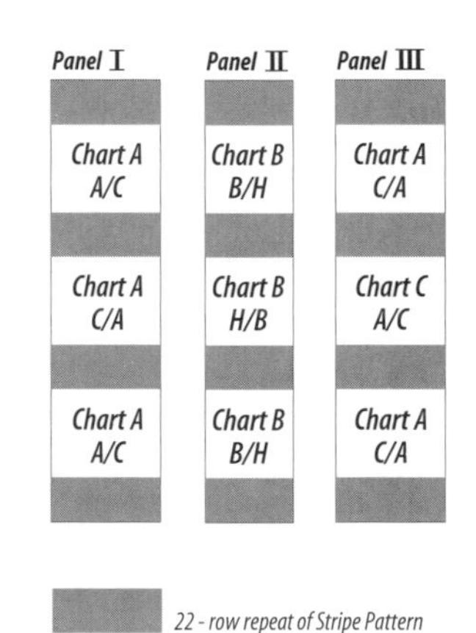

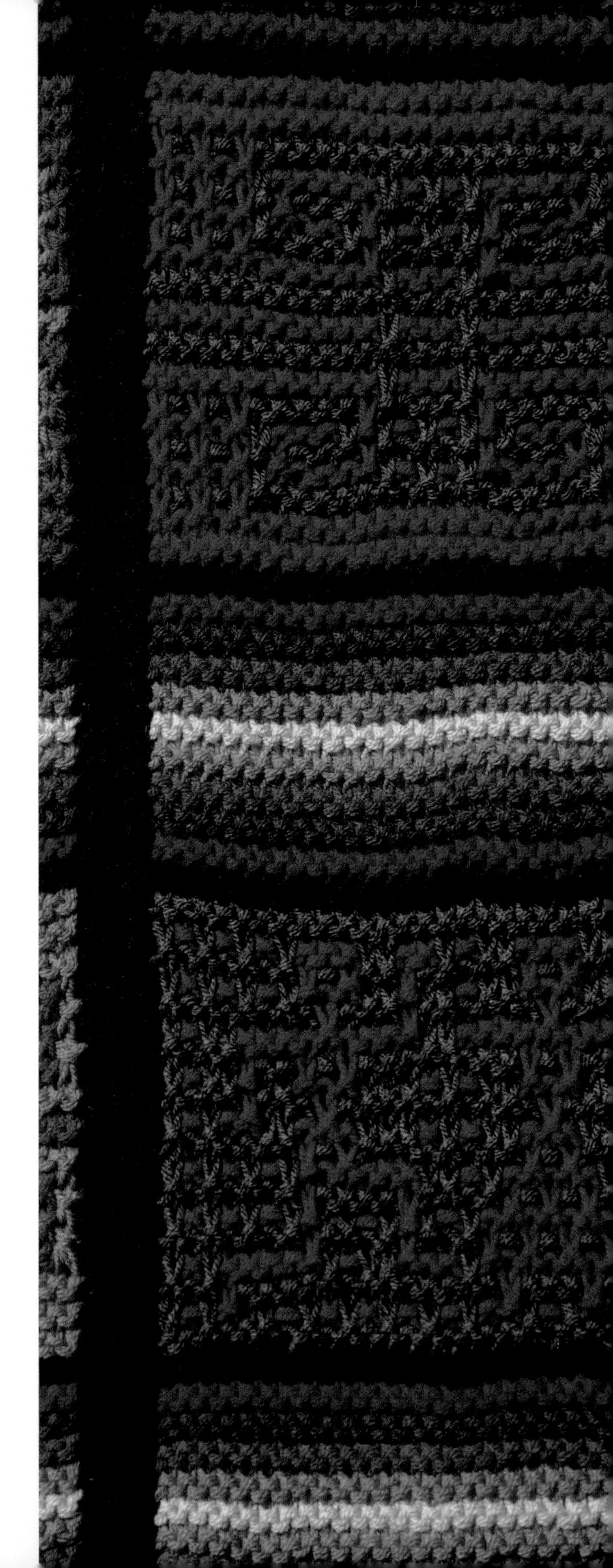

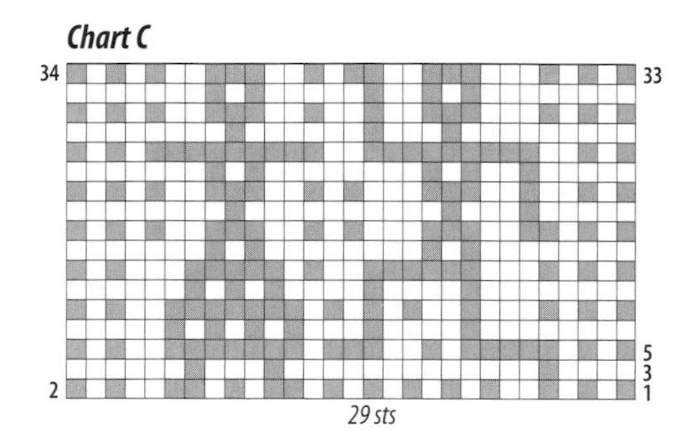

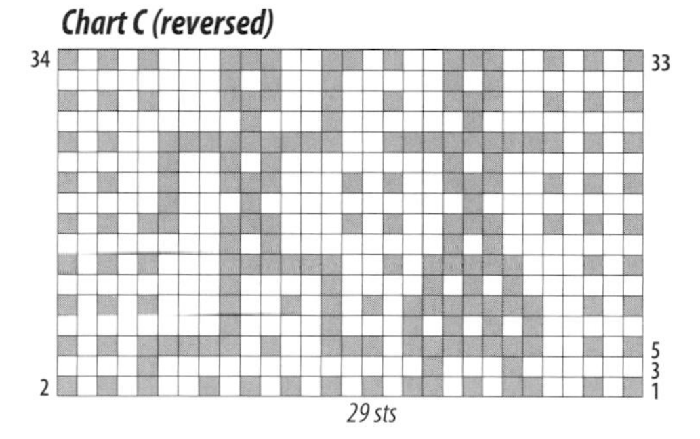

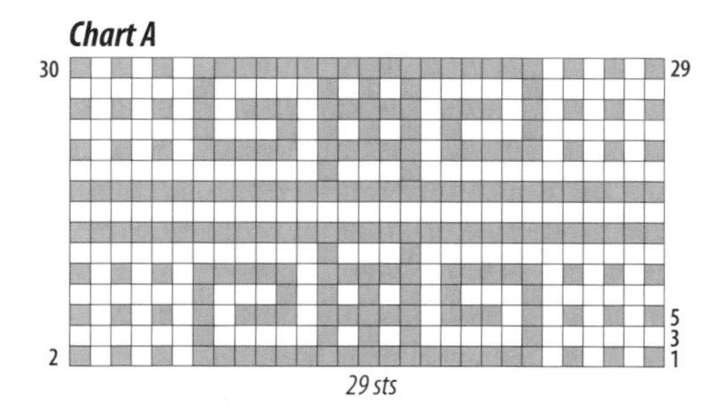

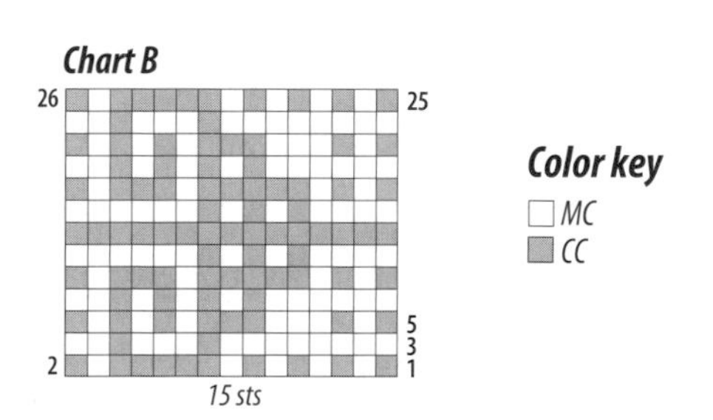

Mosaics the easy way

Mosaic stitch patterns can be worked from abbreviated charts. After a few rows, you will only need to refer to the chart for the RS rows and follow your knitting for the WS rows.

1 Each row represents 2 rows of knitting.

2 Work each row with the color of the first square. Work row 1 (RS) of Charts A, B, and C with CC as follows: reading the chart from right to left, knit the CC stitches (the shaded squares) and slip the MC stitches (the unshaded squares) with the yarn in back.

3 Work row 2 (WS), reading the chart from left to right, knitting the CC stitches and slipping the MC stitches with the yarn in front.

4 Notice that you work both rows with the same color, knitting the same stitches, and slipping the same stitches.

Fine Imitators

Designed by
Knitter's Design Team

EASY +

Pillow
Approximately 16" × 16"

10cm/4"

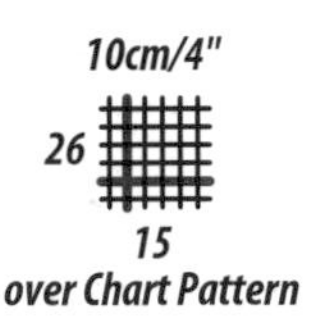

over Chart Pattern

Medium weight
A, B • 80 yds each
C • 85 yds
D, E, F • 65 yds each

• 5.5mm/US 9, or size to obtain gauge
• extra needle for bind off

3.25mm/US D

Five 25mm (1")

&

• stitch holders
• 16" square pillow form

MISSION FALLS 1824 Wool (100% merino wool superwash; 1¾oz/50g; 85yd/78m) in 12 Raisin (A), 28 Pistachio (B), 29 Raspberry (C), 533 Squash (D), 11 Poppy (E), 27 Macaw (F)

Note

See *School*, page 102, for 3-needle bind-off, SSK, slip-stitch crochet, bind off in pattern, and working with double-pointed needles (dpn).

PILLOW

Back

With A, cast on 59 stitches. Work 36 rows of Chart Pattern 3 times. With A, knit 1 row, purl 1 row. Piece measures approximately 17" from beginning. Place stitches on hold.

Front

First Half

With A, cast on 59 stitches. Work 36 rows of Chart Pattern once, then work rows 1–12 once more. Piece measures approximately 7½" from beginning. With C, work in k1, p1 rib for 1". Bind off in rib pattern.

Second Half

With C, cast on 59 stitches. Work in k1, p1 rib for 2", end with a WS row. Work rows 27–36 of Chart Pattern, then work rows 1–36 once more. With A, knit 1 row, purl 1 row. Piece measures approximately 9½" from beginning. Place stitches on hold.

Finishing

Block pieces. With WS facing and A, join open stitches of second half of front and back together, using 3-needle bind-off. With WS facing, crochet hook and A, join cast-on edges of first half of front and back, using slip-stitch crochet. Sew side seams of first half and back. Sew side seams of second half and back, overlapping second half front ribbing over first half front ribbing. Turn right side out and stuff with pillow form. Sew buttons along ribbing, sewing through both thicknesses.

Stitch key
☐ *Knit on RS, purl on WS*
⊟ *Purl on RS*

Color key

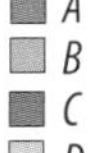

Chart Pattern (pillow)

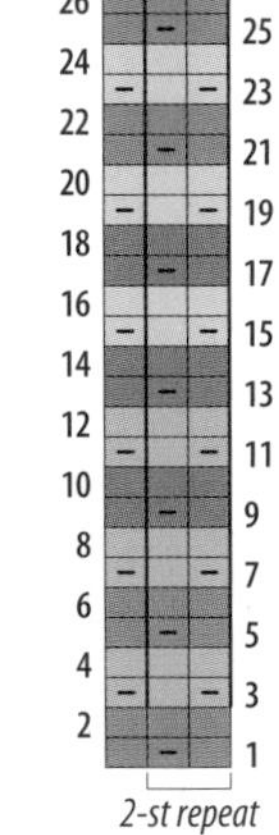

BOLSTER

With circular needle and A, cast on 90 stitches. Place marker (pm) and join, being careful not to twist stitches. Purl 6 rounds. Work 80 rounds of Chart Pattern. Piece measures approximately 14" from beginning (not including rolled edge). With A, purl 6 rounds. Bind off. Block piece.

Ends

With RS facing, circular needle, and A, pick up and knit 90 stitches evenly in purl bumps along inside edge of reverse stockinette stitch edging (see illustration). Pm, join, and work in rounds as follows: ***Round 1*** K2tog, k1, [p2, k2] 21 times, p2tog, p1—88 stitches. ***Rounds 2–8*** [K2, p2] 22 times. ***Round 9*** Slip last purl stitch of round 8 to left needle and with dpn, work as follows: [K2tog, SSK] 22 times—44 stitches. ***Rounds 10–14*** Purl. ***Rounds 15–18*** [K2, p2] 11 times. ***Round 19*** Slip last purl stitch of round 18 to left needle and work as follows: [K2tog, SSK] 11 times—22 stitches. ***Round 20*** [K2tog] 11 times—11 stitches. Cut yarn, run through remaining stitches and pull tightly.Work other end as for first (inserting pillow form after round 8).

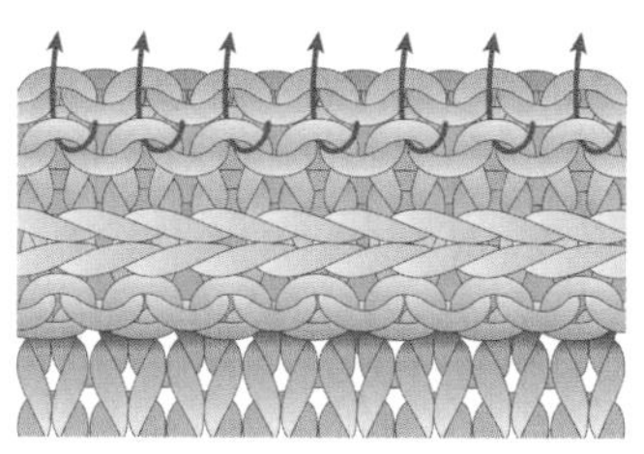

To pick up for ends, fold reverse stockinette stitch edging to front of work and pick up and knit 90 stitches in purl bumps along inside edge (as shown).

Try your own colors online at
www.KnittingUniverse.com/PAINTBOX.

Chart Pattern (bolster)

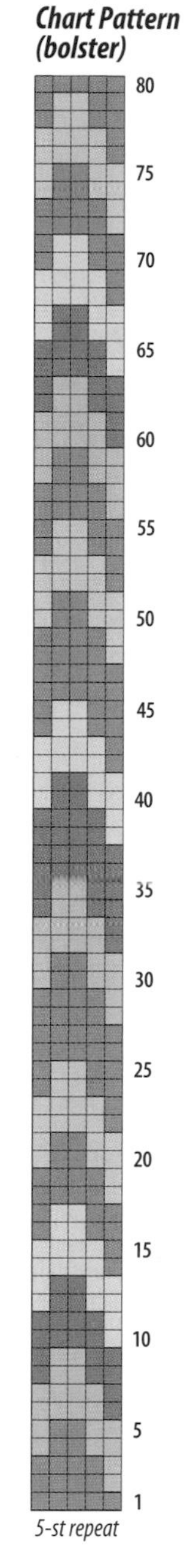

INTERMEDIATE

Bolster
Approximately 14" × 6"

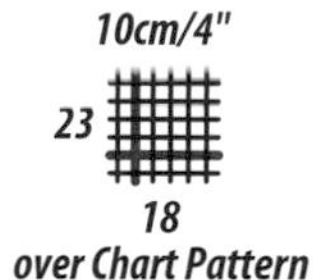

Medium weight
A • 220 yds
B–F • 85 yds each

4.5mm/US 7, or size to obtain gauge, 40cm (16") long

Five 4.5mm/US 7

• stitch markers
• 14" × 6" bolster pillow form

MISSION FALLS 1824 Wool (100% merino wool superwash; 1¾oz/50g; 85yd/78m) in 12 Raisin (A), 28 Pistachio (B), 29 Raspberry (C), 533 Squash (D), 11 Poppy (E), 27 Macaw (F)

Penny Candies

Designed by
Knitter's Design Team

EASY+

Approximately 82½" × 82½"
at widest points

10cm/4"

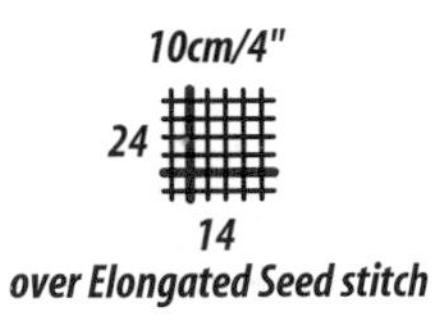

over Elongated Seed stitch

Medium weight
MC • 1,350 yds
CC1, CC2, CC3, CC4 • 155 yds each
CC5, CC6 • 240 yds each
CC7 • 90 yds

6mm/US 10, or size to obtain gauge

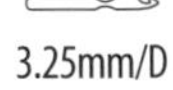

3.25mm/D

MANOS DEL URUGUAY Hand-dyed Wool (100% wool; 3½oz/100g; 138yd/126m) in 100 Agate (MC), 61 Rhubarb (CC1), 49 Henna (CC2), 26 Rosin (CC3), 28 Copper (CC4), U Rust (CC5), W Persimmon (CC6), V Cinnamon (CC7)

Note

See *School*, page 102, for crochet slip-stitch, half double crochet (hdc), 4-in-1 increase, and 3-to-1 decrease.

Elongated Seed Stitch *(Over an odd number of stitches)*

(**Note** Use CC1–7 for rows 3 and 4, as indicated in Afghan instructions.)
Row 1 (RS) With MC, * k1, p1; repeat from *, end k1.
Row 2 With MC, purl.
Row 3 With CC, * p1, k1; repeat from *, end p1.
Row 4 With CC, purl.
Repeat rows 1–4 for Elongated Seed Stitch.

Large Square

With MC, cast on 59 stitches. Work 4 rows of Elongated Seed Stitch 22 times, then work rows 1 and 2 once more. Piece measures approximately 15" from beginning. Bind off with MC.

Small Square

With MC, cast on 31 stitches. Work in Elongated Seed Stitch as follows: Work rows 2–4 once, then repeat rows 1–4 ten times, work rows 1 and 2 once more. Piece measures approximately 7½" from beginning. Bind off with MC.

→ *Direction of knitting*

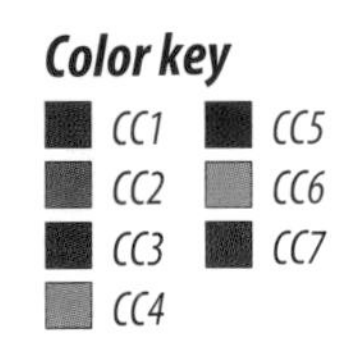

AFGHAN

Make 2 large squares each using CC1, CC2, CC3, and CC4 (8 squares) on rows 3 and 4 of Elongated Seed Stitch. Make 1 large square using CC7.
Make 12 small squares each using CC5 and CC6 (24 squares).

Finishing

Block squares. Assemble squares as shown in diagram and sew together, using MC.

Edging

With RS facing, crochet hook and MC, work 1 round hdc evenly around edge, working a 4-in-1 increase at each outer corner, join last stitch to first with slip stitch. Cut MC. With CC2, work 1 round hdc around edge, working a 4-in-1 increase at each outer corner and a 3-to-1 decrease at each inner corner, join last stitch to first.

Try your own colors online at
www.KnittingUniverse.com/PAINTBOX.

Linen and a Half

Designed by
Knitter's Design Team

EASY+

16" × 16"
16" × 12"

10cm/4"

32/28

17/16
over Linen/Half Linen Stitch

Bulky weight
320/250 yds

5mm/US8, or size to obtain gauge, 60cm/24" long or longer

5.5mm/US9, or size to obtain gauge, 60cm/24" long or longer

&

16" square pillow form

16" × 12" rectangle pillow form
15 yds accent yarn for cord

ROWAN YARNS Kaffe Fassett Colourscape Chunky (100% lambswool; 3 ½oz/100g; 175yd/160m) in 431 Cherry

MALABRIGO YARN Chunky (100% superfine merino wool; 3 ½oz/100g; 104yd/95m) in 207 SM Gold

Notes

1 See *School*, page 102, for 2-color twisted cord. **2** Instructions are given for square and rectangular pillows.

Linen Stitch *(Over an odd number of stitches)*

Row 1 (RS) K1, * yarn to front, slip 1 purlwise, yarn to back, k1; repeat from * to end.
Row 2 (WS) P2, * yarn to back, slip 1 purlwise, yarn to front, p1; repeat from * to last stitch, p1.
Repeat rows 1–2 for Linen Stitch.

Half Linen Stitch *(Over an odd number of stitches)*

Row 1 (RS) K1, * yarn to front, slip 1 purlwise, yarn to back, k1; repeat from * to end.
Row 2 (WS) Purl.
Row 3 K2, * yarn to front, slip 1 purlwise, yarn to back, k1; repeat from *, to last stitch, k1.
Row ***4*** (WS) Purl.
Repeat rows 1–4 for Half Linen Stitch.

Front/Back

Cast on 65 stitches and work Linen (Half Linen) Stitch for 16" (12"). Bind off loosely.

Finishing

Block pieces. Sew front to back along 3 sides. Insert pillow form. Sew remaining side, adding cord if desired.
Optional corded pillow Cut 3½-yard strands: four in pillow color and four in accent color for 2-color twisted cord. Sew 4th side, leaving 1" open at corner. Insert approximately 1" of cord into slit at corner and secure. Attach cord along 4 pillow edges as follows: stitch around cord, following angle of twist. Tuck ends into slit, fasten, sew slit closed.

Stars With Tradition

Designed by
Susan Levin

INTERMEDIATE

Small 12" × 12"
Large 15" × 15"

10cm/4"

20

16

over stockinette stitch (knit on RS, purl on WS), using 2 strands of yarn held together throughout

Medium weight
Large pillow
MC • 220 yds
A, B, C, D • 90 yds each
Small pillow
MC • 200 yds
CC • 150 yds

4.5mm/US 7, or size to obtain gauge

• yarn bobbin
• square pillow forms: 12" or 14"

NASHUA HANDKINTS Creative Focus Worsted (75% wool, 25% alpaca; 3½oz/100g; 220 yds/200m) in 500 Ebony (MC) Velvet Wool (88% wool, 12% nylon; .875oz/25g; 82yd/75m) in 4053 Lavender (A), 1460 Juniper (B), 3812 Pale Violet (C), 1940 Dried Rose (D)

Notes

1 See *School*, page 102, for 2-color twisted cord and intarsia. **2** When changing colors, twist yarns on WS to prevent holes. **3** Use small balls of yarn for large areas of color. **4** Use 2 strands of yarn held together throughout.

Large pillow *(Make 2)*

With MC, cast on 59 stitches. Purl 1 row. Working in stockinette stitch and first color sequence, work rows 1–20 of Chart A. Repeat rows 3–20 a total of 3 times more, working in color sequence as indicated. Bind off.

Small pillow

With MC, cast on 47 stitches. Working in stockinette stitch, work 58 rows of Chart B, using C for star motif. In same way, make 2nd piece using D for star motif.

Chart A

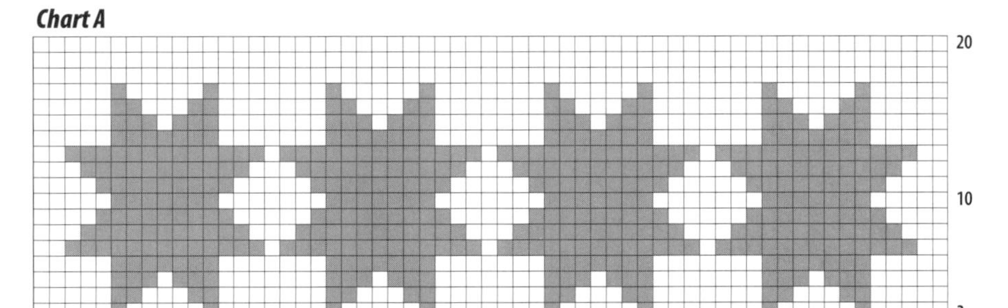

Color sequence

A	B	D	C
C	D	A	B
B	A	C	D
D	C	B	A

Color key
A *Lavender*
B *Juniper*
C *Pale Violet*
D *Dried Rose*

Work 4 repeats of Chart A, using A, B, C, and D as CC.

Stitch key

Chart B

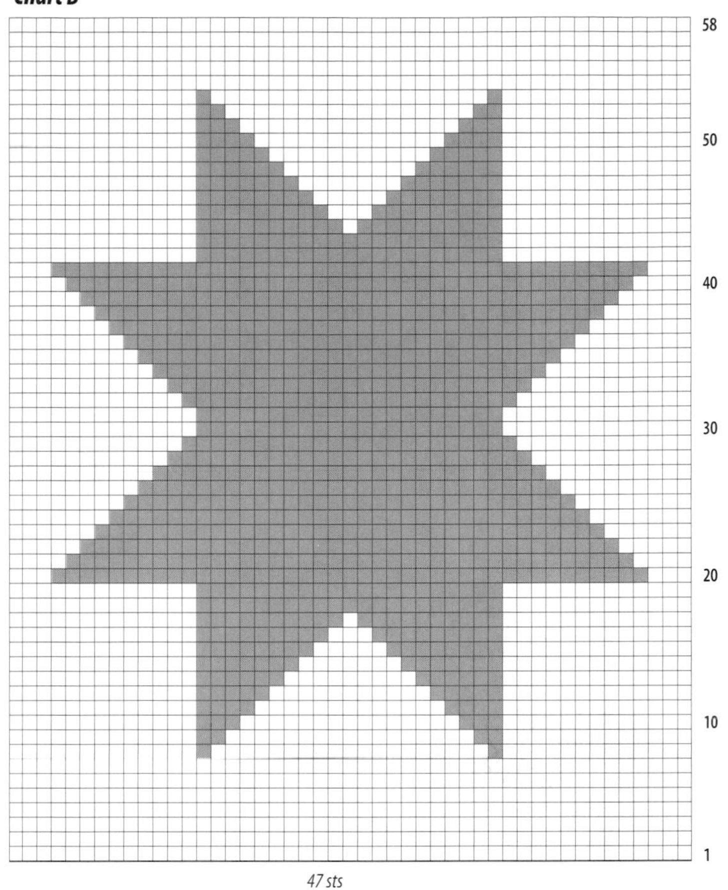

Finishing

Block pieces lightly. With WS facing, sew 3 sides together. Turn RS out and insert pillow form. Sew 4th side, leaving 1" open at corner. Insert approximately 1" of cord into slit at corner and secure. With MC, attach cord along 4 pillow edges as follows: stitch around cord, following angle of twist. Tuck ends into slit, fasten, sew slit closed.

2-color twisted cord

Small (large) pillow

Cut 3 (3½) yard strands as follows: one each in A, B, C, and D (to be held together) and 4 strands of MC (to be held together).

Try your own colors online at
www.KnittingUniverse.com/PAINTBOX.

Star Afghan

Designed by
Sandra Daignault

INTERMEDIATE +

Approximately 50" diameter

10cm/4"

28 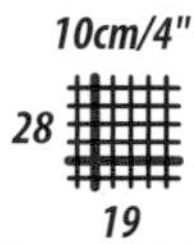

19

over Garter Ridge Pattern

For gauge swatch, with larger needles, work back and forth in rows as follows: ***Rows 1, 3, 5 and 7*** (RS) Knit. ***Row 2*** (WS) Purl. ***Row 4*** Knit. ***Rows 6 and 8*** Purl. Repeat rows 1–8.

Light weight
1200 yds

4.5mm/US 7, or size to obtain gauge, 40cm (16"), 60cm (24"), and 100cm (40") long

four each 4mm/US 6 and 4.5mm/US 7

stitch marker

COATS MODA DEA Sassy Stripes (100% acrylic; 1¾oz/50g; 147yd/135m) in 6980 Rave

Notes

1 See *School*, page 102, for S2KP2, circle cast-on, KOK, and working with double-pointed needles (dpn). **2** Change to 16", 24", and 40" circular needles as needed. **3** Consult table for number of knit stitches to work between KOK's and S2KP2's on odd-numbered rounds of Garter Ridge Pattern. Work each repeat 10 times.

Afghan

Circle cast on 7 stitches. Divide stitches among 3 smaller dpn. Place marker, join and work in rounds as follows: ***Begin Center Pattern: Round 1*** Yarn over (yo), [k1, k1 through back loop] 3 times, k1—8 stitches. ***Round 2*** [K1, yo] 7 times, k1—15 stitches. ***Rounds 3 and 4*** Knit. ***Round 5*** [K1, yo] 15 times—30 stitches. ***Rounds 6–9*** Knit. ***Round 10*** [K1, yo] 30 times—60 stitches. ***Rounds 11 and 12*** Knit. Change to larger dpn.

Begin Circular Garter Ridge Pattern: Round 1 [KOK, **k1**, S2KP2, k1] 10 times. ***Round 2*** Move marker (mm) 1 stitch to left as follows: Remove marker, slip 1, replace marker, knit to end. ***Round 3*** [KOK, **k5**] 10 times—80 stitches. ***Round 4*** Mm, purl to end. ***Round 5*** [KOK, **k2**, S2KP2, k2] 10 times. ***Rounds 6 and 8*** Repeat round 2. ***Round 7*** [KOK, **k7**] 10 times—100 stitches. ***Round 9*** [KOK, **k3**, S2KP2, k3] 10 times. ***Round 10*** Repeat round 2. ***Round 11*** [KOK, **k9**] 10 times—120 stitches. ***Round 12*** Repeat round 4. ***Round 13*** [KOK, **k4**, S2KP2, k4] 10 times. ***Round 14*** Repeat round 2. ***Round 15*** [KOK, **k11**] 10 times—140 stitches. ***Round 16*** Repeat round 2. Continue in pattern as established through round 128, consulting table for number of knit stitches to work between KOK's and S2KP2's on odd-numbered rounds.

Finishing

Edging

Round 1 [KOK, **k33**, S2KP2, k33] 10 times. ***Round 2*** Mm, knit to end. ***Round 3*** [KOK, **k69**] 10 times. ***Rounds 4 and 6*** Mm, purl to end. ***Round 5*** [KOK, **k34**, S2KP2, k34] 10 times. ***Round 7*** [KOK, **k71**] 10 times. ***Round 8*** Purl. Bind off.

Circular Garter Ridge Pattern

	1 ▲ 1 ∨	***Rnd 1***
80 sts	5 ∨	***Rnd 3***
	2 ▲ 2 ∨	***Rnd 5***
100 sts	7 ∨	***Rnd 7***
	3 ▲ 3 ∨	***Rnd 9***
120 sts	9 ∨	***Rnd 11***
	4 ▲ 4 ∨	***Rnd 13***
140 sts	11 ∨	***Rnd 15***
	5 ▲ 5 ∨	***Rnd 17***
160 sts	13 ∨	***Rnd 19***
	6 ▲ 6 ∨	***Rnd 21***
180 sts	15 ∨	***Rnd 23***
	7 ▲ 7 ∨	***Rnd 25***
200 sts	17 ∨	***Rnd 27***
	8 ▲ 8 ∨	***Rnd 29***
220 sts	19 ∨	***Rnd 31***
	9 ▲ 9 ∨	***Rnd 33***
240 sts	21 ∨	***Rnd 35***
	10 ▲ 10 ∨	***Rnd 37***
260 sts	23 ∨	***Rnd 39***
	11 ▲ 11 ∨	***Rnd 41***
280 sts	25 ∨	***Rnd 43***
	12 ▲ 12 ∨	***Rnd 45***
300 sts	27 ∨	***Rnd 47***
	13 ▲ 13 ∨	***Rnd 49***
320 sts	29 ∨	***Rnd 51***
	14 ▲ 14 ∨	***Rnd 53***
340 sts	31 ∨	***Rnd 55***
	15 ▲ 15 ∨	***Rnd 57***
360 sts	33 ∨	***Rnd 59***
	16 ▲ 16 ∨	***Rnd 61***
380 sts	35 ∨	***Rnd 63***
	17 ▲ 17 ∨	***Rnd 65***
400 sts	37 ∨	***Rnd 67***
	18 ▲ 18 ∨	***Rnd 69***
420 sts	39 ∨	***Rnd 71***
	19 ▲ 19 ∨	***Rnd 73***
440 sts	41 ∨	***Rnd 75***
	20 ▲ 20 ∨	***Rnd 77***
460 sts	43 ∨	***Rnd 79***
	21 ▲ 21 ∨	***Rnd 81***
480 sts	45 ∨	***Rnd 83***
	22 ▲ 22 ∨	***Rnd 85***
500 sts	47 ∨	***Rnd 87***
	23 ▲ 23 ∨	***Rnd 89***
520 sts	49 ∨	***Rnd 91***
	24 ▲ 24 ∨	***Rnd 93***
540 sts	51 ∨	***Rnd 95***
	25 ▲ 25 ∨	***Rnd 97***
560 sts	53 ∨	***Rnd 99***
	26 ▲ 26 ∨	***Rnd 101***
580 sts	55 ∨	***Rnd 103***
	27 ▲ 27 ∨	***Rnd 105***
600 sts	57 ∨	***Rnd 107***
	28 ▲ 28 ∨	***Rnd 109***
620 sts	59 ∨	***Rnd 111***
	29 ▲ 29 ∨	***Rnd 113***
640 sts	61 ∨	***Rnd 115***
	30 ▲ 30 ∨	***Rnd 117***
660 sts	63 ∨	***Rnd 119***
	31 ▲ 31 ∨	***Rnd 121***
680 sts	65 ∨	***Rnd 123***
	32 ▲ 32 ∨	***Rnd 125***
700 sts	67 ∨	***Rnd 127***

Edging

	33 ▲ 33 ∨	***Rnd 1***
720 sts	69 ∨	***Rnd 3***
	34 ▲ 34 ∨	***Rnd 5***
740 sts	71 ∨	***Rnd 7***

Stitch key

▲ *S2KP2*
∨ *KOK*

Wild Country Cushions

Designed by
Knitter's Design Team

EASY +
One size
14" × 14"

10cm/4"
22
16
over stockinette stitch (knit every round)

Bulky weight
MC • 270 yds each
CC • 135 yds each

• 6mm/US 10, or size to obtain gauge, 60cm/24" long
• extra needle for bind-off

• tapestry needle
• stitch marker
• 14" square pillow form

MANOS DEL URUGUAY (100% wool; 3½oz/100g; 135yd/123m)
Zebra: 14 Natural (MC) and 8 Black (CC1)
Leopard: 40 Goldenrod (MC), 37 Thrush (CC1) and 8 Black (CC2)
Giraffe: 28 Copper (MC) and V Cinnamon (CC1)

NOTE

See *School*, page 102, for 3-needle bind-off.

PILLOW

With MC, cast on 112 stitches. Place marker and join, being careful not to twist stitches. Knit every round for 74 rounds. Piece measures approximately 13½" from beginning. Leave stitches on needle.

Finishing

Turn pillow inside out. With extra needle, join seam using 3-needle bind-off. Work duplicate stitch on front following chart (placing pattern as desired within 56 stitches). Insert pillow form, sew other seam.

DUPLICATE STITCH
Duplicate stitch is just that: with a blunt tapestry needle threaded with a length of yarn of a contrasting color, cover a knitted stitch with an embroidered stitch of the same shape.

Color key
☐ *MC*
■ *CC1*
■ *CC2*

Zebra Chart

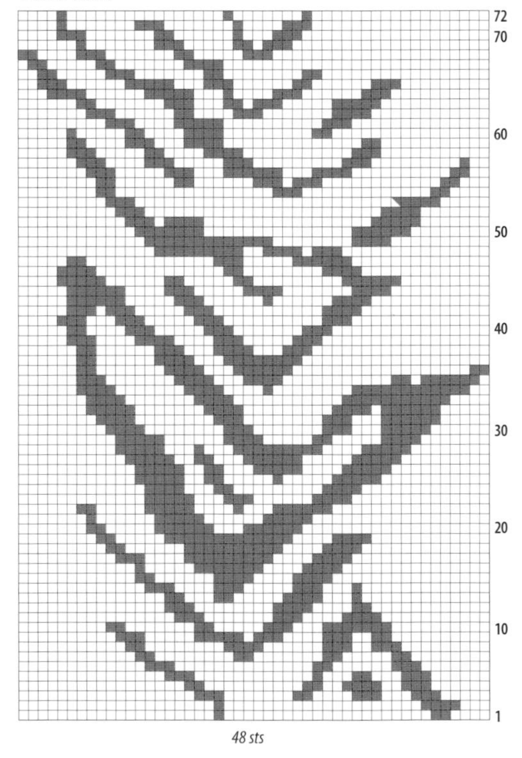

Giraffe Chart

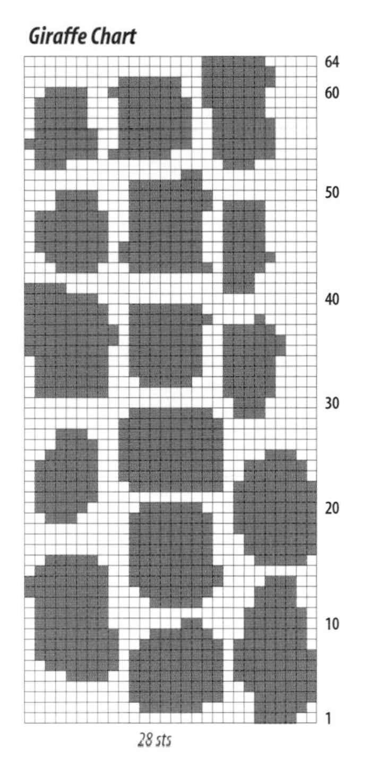

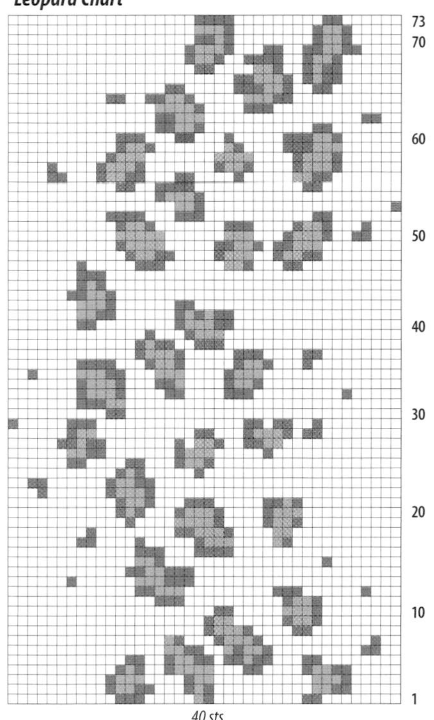

Textures at Home

Frosted Counterpanes

Designed by
Heather Lodinsky

EASY

47½" × 55" at widest point

10cm/4"

18

13

over stockinette stitch (knit on RS, purl on WS)

1 2 3 4 5 6

Bulky weight
2250 yds

6.5mm/US 10½, or size to obtain gauge, 60cm/24" long

four 6.5mm/US 10½

- stitch marker
- tapestry needle

BROWN SHEEP Lamb's Pride Bulky (85% wool, 15% mohair; 4 oz/113g; 125 yds/114m) in M-11 White Frost

Note

Change to double-pointed needles (dpn) when necessary.

Hexagon *(Make 32)*

With circular needle, cast on 120 stitches. Place marker and join, being careful not to twist stitches. ***Begin Chart Pattern: Round 1*** Work 20-stitch repeat around—108 stitches. Work through chart round 21—6 stitches. Draw yarn through remaining stitches, pull together tightly and fasten off.

Finishing

Block hexagons.

Following diagrams on page 40, embroider 8 hexagons each of A, B, C, and D. Sew hexagons together, following assembly diagram.

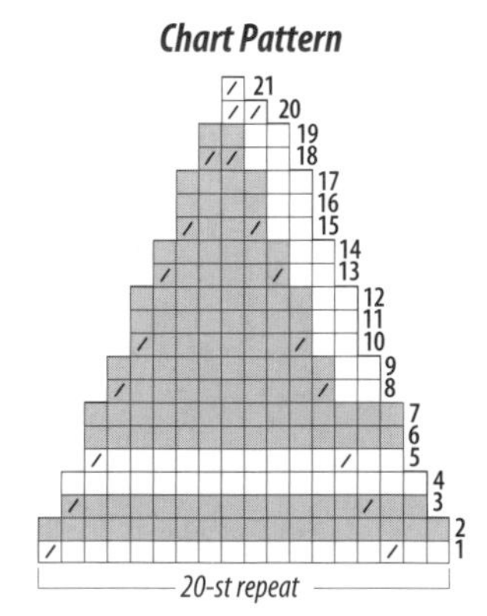

LAZY DAISY

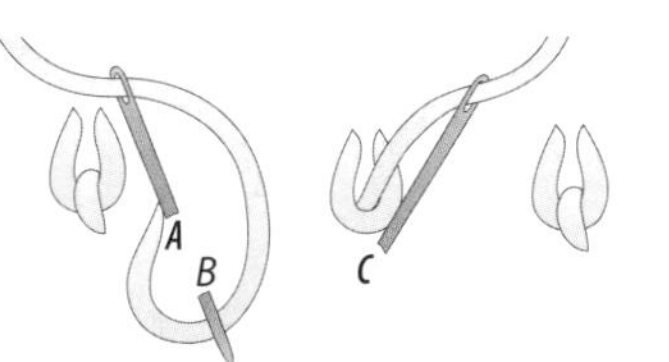

FRENCH KNOT

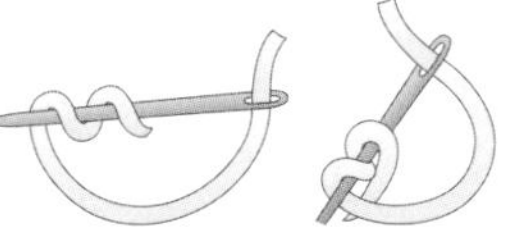

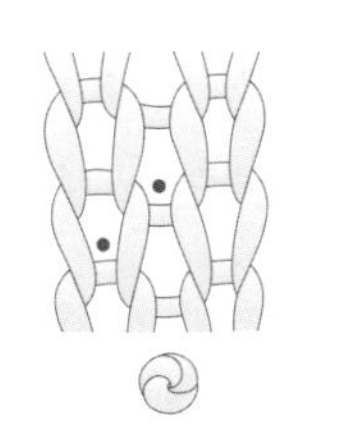

CHAIN STITCH

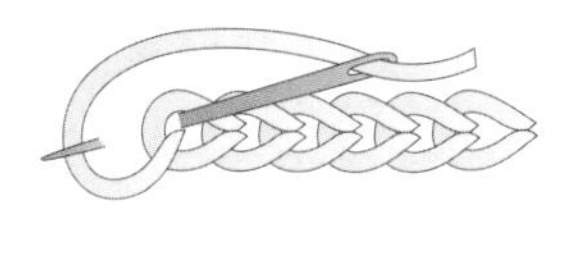

Assembly diagram

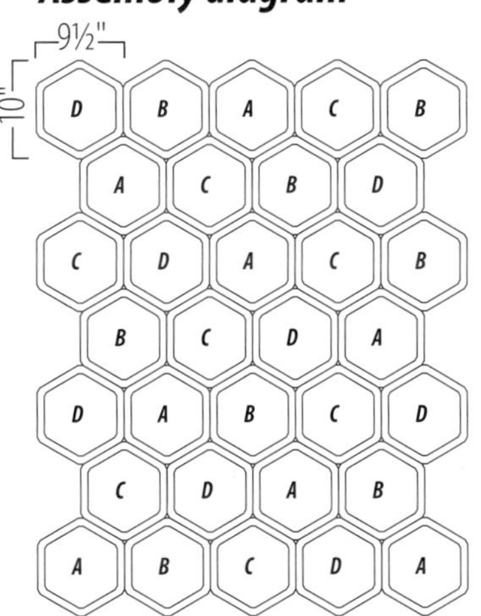

Next page, Leafy lace, instructions follow.

Leafy Lace

Designed by
Gitta Schrade

INTERMEDIATE

Afghan 43" × 67" including edging
Pillow 17" × 16" without edging

10cm/4" ***14.5cm/5¾"***

32

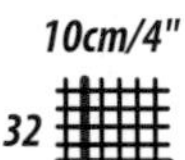

29

For gauge swatch, using larger needle, cast on 29 stitches and work 16 rows of Chart A twice. Your swatch should measure 5¾" wide by 4" high.

Medium weight
Afghan • 2730 yds
Pillow • 840 yds

Afghan • 3.75mm/US 5, or size to obtain gauge, 100cm/40" long

Pillow • 3.25mm/US 3 and 3.75mm/ US 5

16" square pillow form

PATONS Decor (75% acrylic, 25% wool; 3½oz/100g; 210yd/192m) in 1602 Ecru

Note

See *School*, page 102, for SSK, SK2P, SSP, k1 tbl, p1 tbl, yo before a knit and purl stitch.

AFGHAN

Cast on 185 stitches. Work 16 rows of Chart A 32 times. Bind off.

Finishing

Block piece lightly.

Long edging (Make 2)

Cast on 310 stitches. Work 12 rows of Chart B. Bind off in pattern.

Short edging (Make 2)

Cast on 190 stitches. Work as for long edge.

Sew edgings to afghan. Sew mitred corners. Block seams lightly. Embroider one flower in each corner, using satin stitch for leaves, and pulling up a stitch and working bobble for flower.

PILLOW

Front

With larger needles, cast on 81 stitches. Work 16 rows of Chart A 8 times. Bind off.

Back *(Make 2)*

With larger needles, cast on 80 stitches. Work 7¼" in stockinette stitch (knit on RS, purl on WS). Change to smaller needles. Work 1½" in k1, p1 rib. Bind off in rib.

Finishing

Block pieces lightly. Sew first back piece to front with ribbed edge at center. Sew 2nd piece, overlapping ribbed edges at center.

Ruffled edging (Make 4)

With larger needles, cast on 69 stitches. Work 6 rows in garter stitch (knit every row), increasing 1 stitch each side on first 5 rows—79 stitches. Work 10 rows of Chart C. Bind off in pattern.

Sew edging to pillow. Sew mitred corners.

Make leaf (Worked on row 9 of Chart B and row 7 of Chart C)
[Insert tip of right needle between knit stitch and k1 tbl stitch on row 2 of Chart B (or row 1 of Chart C), pull yarn through and up to working row, yo] 3 times—6 stitches; place left needle into fronts of all 6 stitches from left to right and knit them together.

Bobble
[(K1, yo) 4 times, k1] into stitch; slip loops one by one over last loop and off needle.

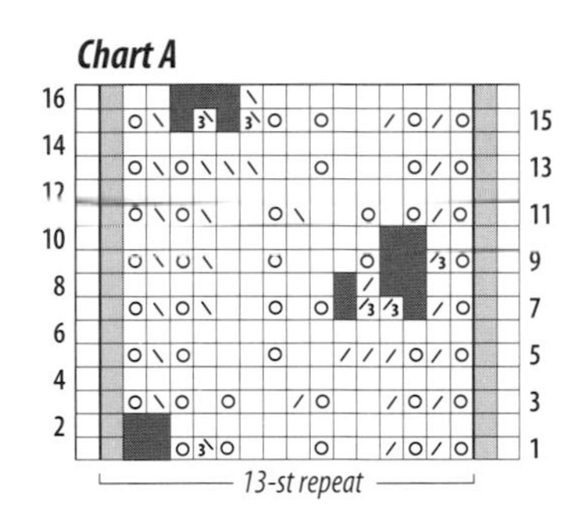

Stitch key

- *Knit on RS, purl on WS*
- *Purl on RS, knit on WS*
- *Yarn over (yo)*
- *K2tog on RS, p2tog on WS*
- *SSK on RS, SSP on WS*
- *SK2P*
- *K3tog*
- *Stitches do not exist in these areas of chart*
- *K1 tbl on RS, p1 tbl on WS*
- *Make bobble*
- *Purl into front and back of stitch*
- *Make leaf*

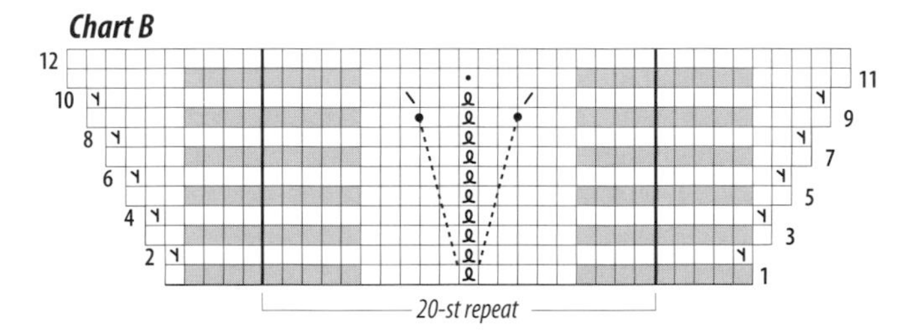

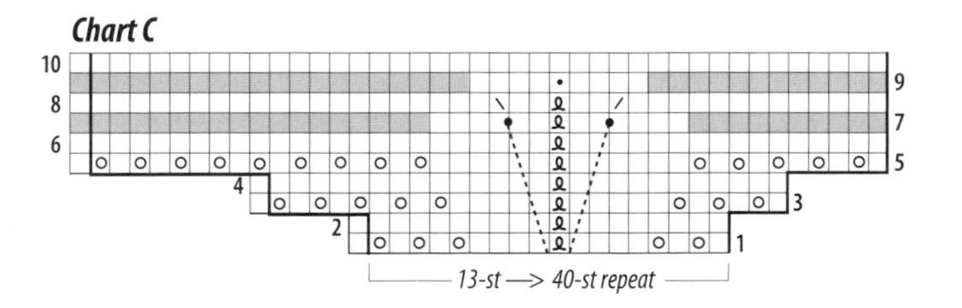

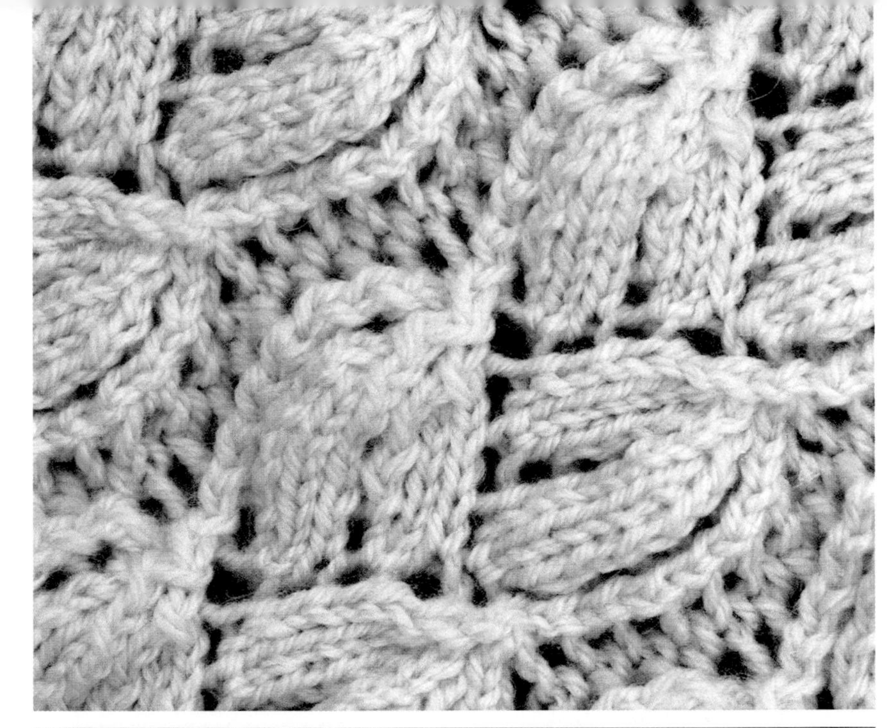

Pita Pillow

Designed by
Paula Levy

INTERMEDIATE

Approximately 14" diameter

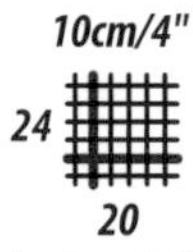

over stockinette stitch (knit on RS, purl on WS)

Medium weight
300 yds

4mm/US 6, or size to obtain gauge
a pair of smaller sized needles (or a circular) for seaming

3.75mm/F

- cable needle (cn)
- 14" diameter pillow form

BROWN SHEEP Lamb's Pride SuperWash (100% wool; 1¾oz/50g; 100yds/90m) in SW20 Rose Blush

Note

See *School*, page 102, for M1L, M1R, S2KP2, SSK, and SSSK.

PILLOW WEDGES (Make 5)

Front

Cast on 3 stitches.

Work Wedge chart rows 1–45 — 47 sts.

Folding ridge

Rows 46 & 48 (WS) Knit.

Row 47 (RS) K1, p45, k1.

Back

Row 49 K1, k2tog, knit until 3 stitches remain, SSK, k1. ***Row 50 & all even (WS) rows*** K1, purl until 1 stitch remains, k1. ***Row 51*** Repeat row 49. ***Row 53*** K1, k3tog, knit until 4 stitches remain, SSSK, k1. ***Rows 55 & 57*** Repeat row 49. ***Row 59*** Repeat row 53. ***Rows 61 & 63*** Repeat row 49. ***Row 65*** Repeat row 53. ***Rows 67–83 (RS rows)*** Repeat row 49. ***Row 85*** K1, S2KP2, k1. End with Row 86. Bind off remaining 3 stitches.

Join wedges with a linked seam, leaving an opening to insert pillow form.

Finishing

Block to 14" diameter, making sure seams and travelling ribs are straight. Insert pillow form and sew opening closed.

Wedge Chart

Note: After row 45, do not bind off. Follow instructions for Folding Ridge and Back.

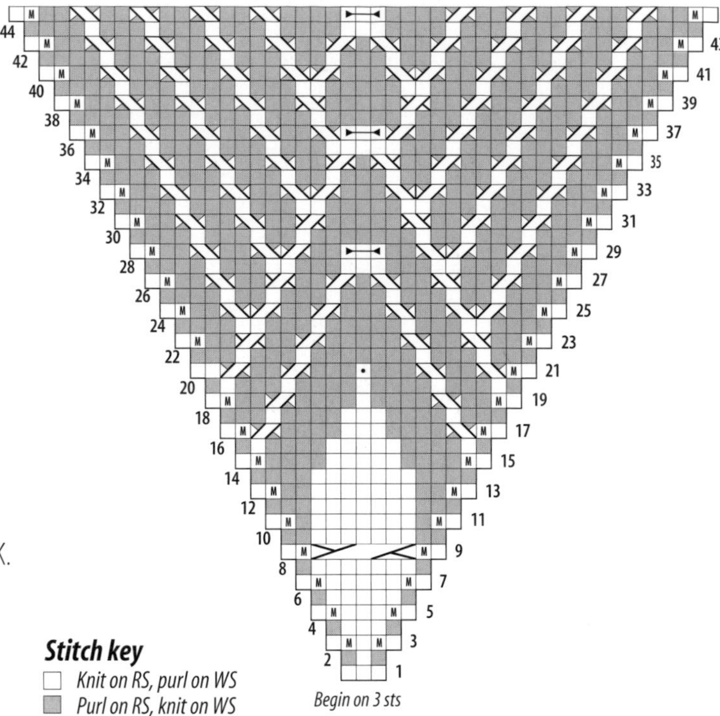

Begin on 3 sts

Stitch key

- *Knit on RS, purl on WS*
- *Purl on RS, knit on WS*
- M ***M1*** *Work M1R at beginning of row and M1L at end of row*
- • *Make bobble*
- ***1/1 RPC*** *Slip 1 to cn and hold in back, k1, p1 from cn*
- ***1/1 LPC*** *Slip 1 to cn and hold in front, p1, k1 from cn*
- ***1/1 RC*** *Slip 1 to cn and hold in back, k1, k1 from cn*
- ***1/1 LC*** *Slip 1 to cn and hold in front, k1, k1 from cn*
- ***Cluster 3*** *Slip 3 to cn, wrap yarn clockwise around the 3 sts 3 times, ending in back. K3 from cn*
- ***4/3 RC*** *Slip 3 to cn and hold in back, k4, k3 from cn*

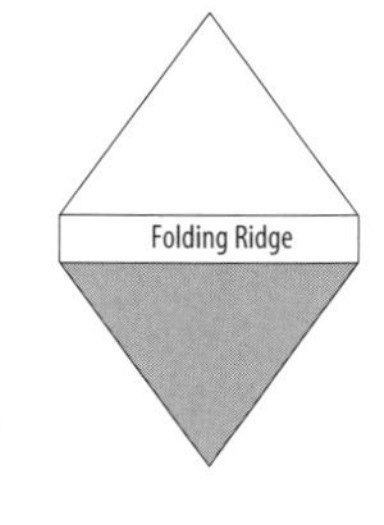

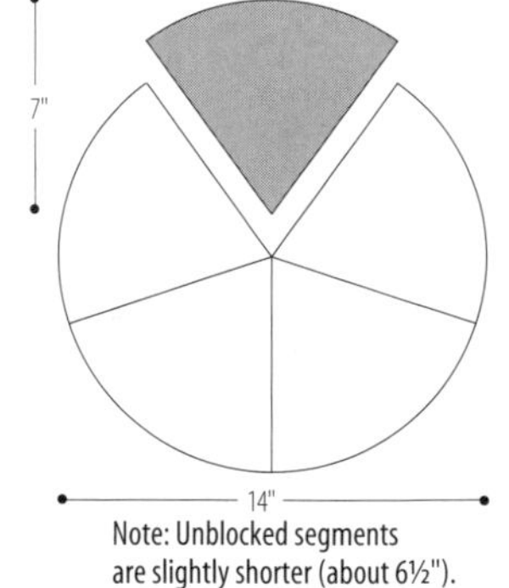

Note: Unblocked segments are slightly shorter (about 6½").

MAKE BOBBLE

(K1, k1 tbl, k1, k1 tbl, k1) in 1 stitch, turn, p5, turn, (slip 1 knitwise) 5 times, (pass second stitch on right needle over first stitch) 4 times, transferring the slack from stitch to stitch as each stitch is passed over. Finally, tighten the remaining stitch.

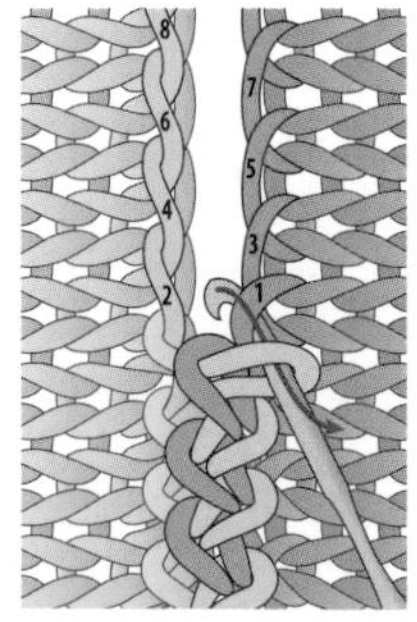

LINKING A SEAM

Place pieces side by side, with RS facing you.

1 With crochet hook, catch loop at lower corner of piece.

2 Roll hook, catch loop from opposite piece and pull through loop on hook.

Repeat Step 2 until 1 loop remains on hook. Secure the last loop with an available end or an extra piece of yarn. Seam is neat and attractive on both sides.

Tulips in the Sand

Designed by
Paula Levy

INTERMEDIATE

approximately 28" × 43"

10cm/4"

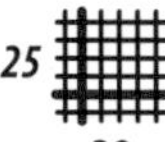

25

20

over stockinette stitch (knit on RS, purl on WS), unblocked

1 2 3 **4** 5 6

Medium weight
1075 yds

4.5mm/US 7, or size to obtain gauge

4.25mm/G

- cable needle (cn)
- cotton swab
- blocking pins

BROWN SHEEP Cotton Fleece (80% cotton, 20% wool; 3½oz/100g; 215yds/194m) in CW570 Malibu Blue

Note

See *School,* page 102, for S2KP2, M1L, M1R, loop cast-on, lifted increase, and slip stitch crochet.

Tulip square *(Make 24)*

Using loop cast-on, cast on 3 stitches. Work rows 1–30 of Chart A—33 stitches. Then work rows 1–42 of Chart B. Bind off remaining 3 stitches.

Finishing

Block each tulip to an 8" square. Use a cotton swab to puff the tulips. The squares will relax back to about 7¼" when unpinned.
Sew tulip squares together in 4 strips of 6 squares each following Joining Diagram for placement, then sew strips together.

Slip-stitch border

With RS facing, crochet hook, and starting left of a corner, work slip stitch crochet around the throw, working an extra slip stitch at each corner. Work a second round of slip stitches into the same spaces as the first round. Cut the yarn and draw through the last loop.

Joining diagram

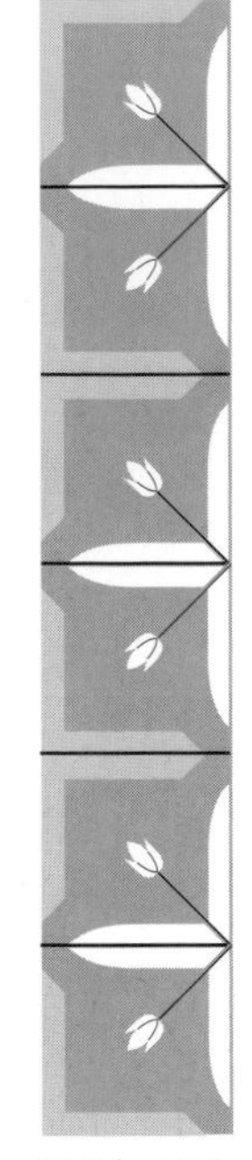

Join tulips into 6-square stripes.

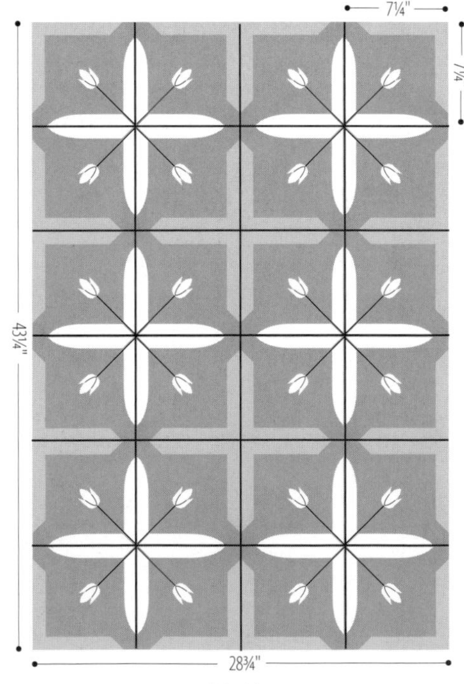

Join strips.

Four Sisters Afghan

Designed by
Paula Levy

INTERMEDIATE+

48" × 64"

10cm/4"

27 / 23
over stockinette stitch (knit on RS, purl on WS)

1 2 3 4 5 6

Light weight
2365 yds

3.5mm/US 4, or size to obtain gauge

3.5mm/E

tapestry needle

LANE BORGOSESIA Knitaly (100% superwash wool; 3½oz/100g; 215yd/193m) in 315 Ice Blue Heather

Note

See *School*, page 102, for SSK, SSP, k3tog, p3tog, slip-stitch crochet, and S2KP2.

Triangle

Make 48 triangles following Triangle Chart on page 50.

Finishing

Block triangles to measurements: working from cast-on to bound-off edge, make sure that sides A & B are at right angles to each other. Side C will relax back to 16" when dry.

Blocking measurements

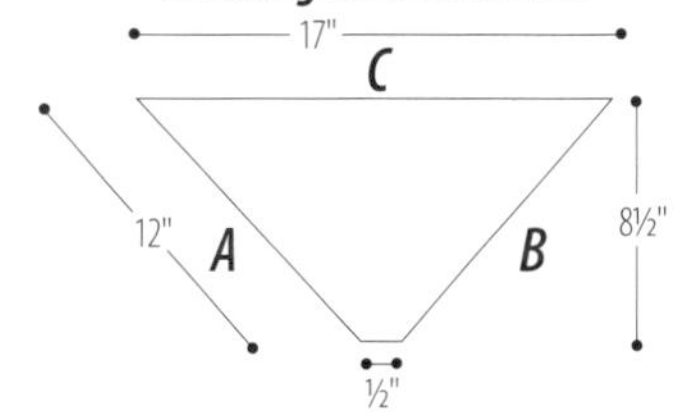

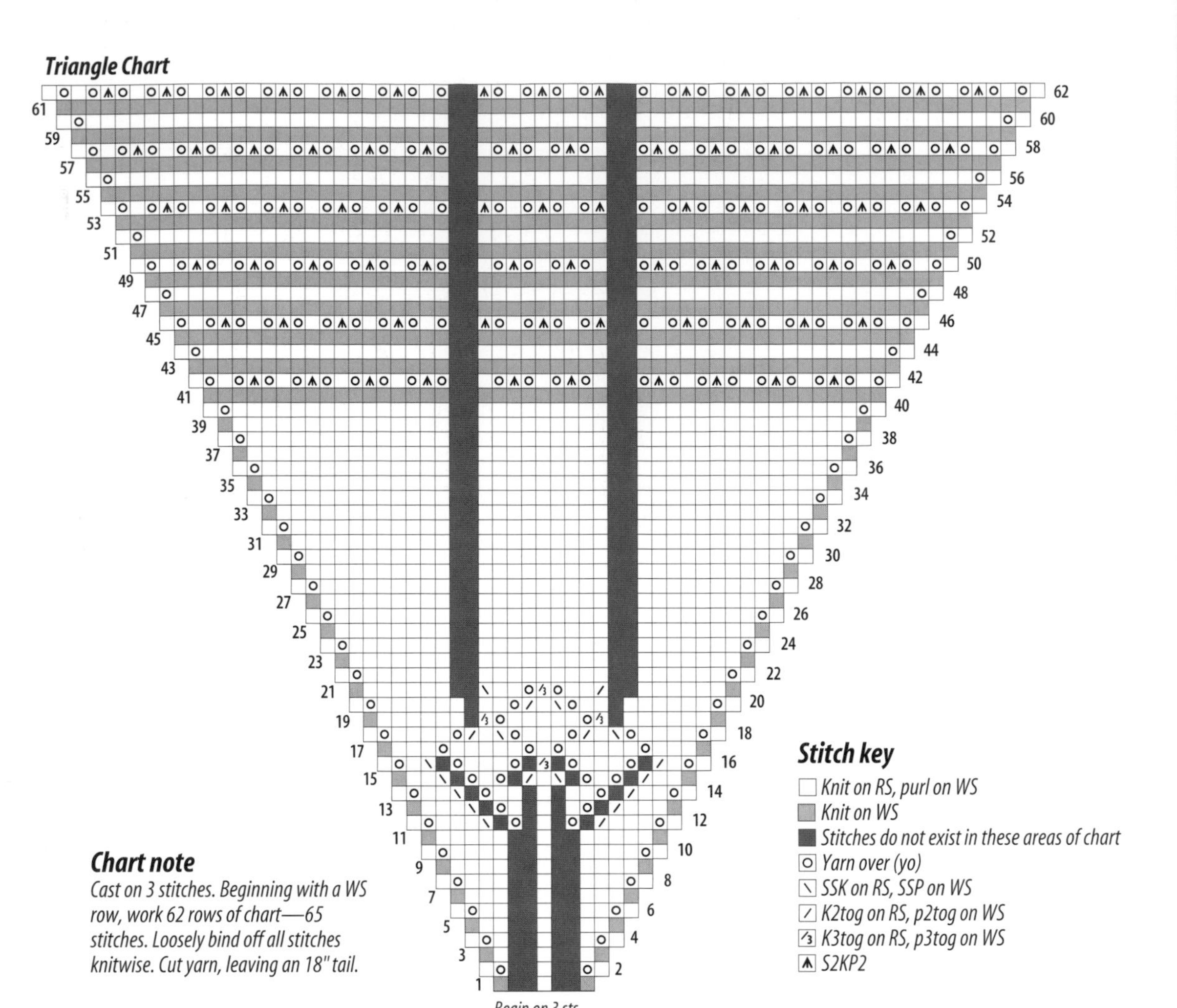

Assemble triangles into 12 squares

Arrange 4 triangles into a square, cast-on points in the center and matching side A to side B of neighboring triangles. Seam using tails and working from bound-off edges to center.

Join squares

* Line up 2 squares to be joined, marking center of side C on each square. Beginning at markers and leaving a 17" tail, work overcast stitch through the upper strands of the bind-off chains to end. Sew seam from center in other direction to complete join. Join 2 more squares to form a strip of 4 squares. Repeat from * 2 more times—3 strips. Join 3 strips to form afghan, taking an extra stitch from each side at cross seams. Knot ends from cross seams to secure before weaving them in.

Crochet border

With RS facing, join yarn to one corner and work slip-stitch crochet around edge of afghan, working an extra stitch at each corner and 2 or 3 extra at the seams.

Joining Diagram

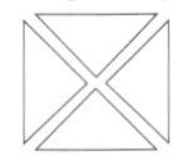

Join triangles into 4-triangle squares.

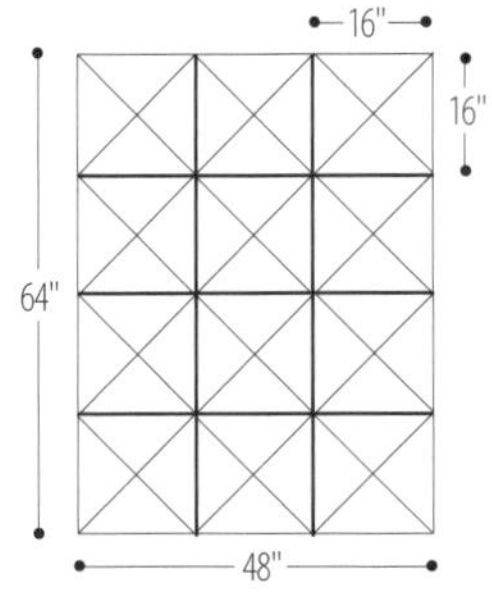

Join squares into three 4-square strips. Join strips.

Stitch key

- ☐ Knit on RS, purl on WS
- ▩ Purl on RS, knit on WS
- M **M1:** M1L at beginning of row, M1R at end
- K1, p1, k1, p1, k1 in one st
- RLI, k1, LLI, **see illustration**
- R RLI, k1
- L K1, LLI
- \ SSK
- / K2tog
- ⋀ S2KP2
- Slip 1 purlwise with yarn in front
- **1/1 LPC** Slip 1 to cn, hold to front, p1, k1 from cn
- **1/1 RPC** Slip 1 to cn, hold to back, k1, p1 from cn

Chart note

Using loop cast-on, cast on 3 stitches.
Work rows 1–30 of Chart A—33 stitches.
Then work rows 1–42 of Chart B.
Bind off remaining 3 stitches.

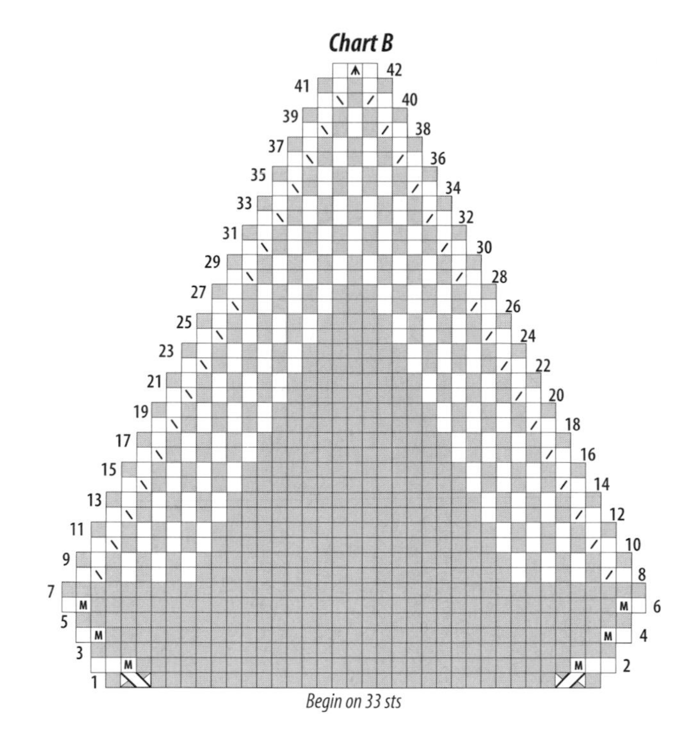

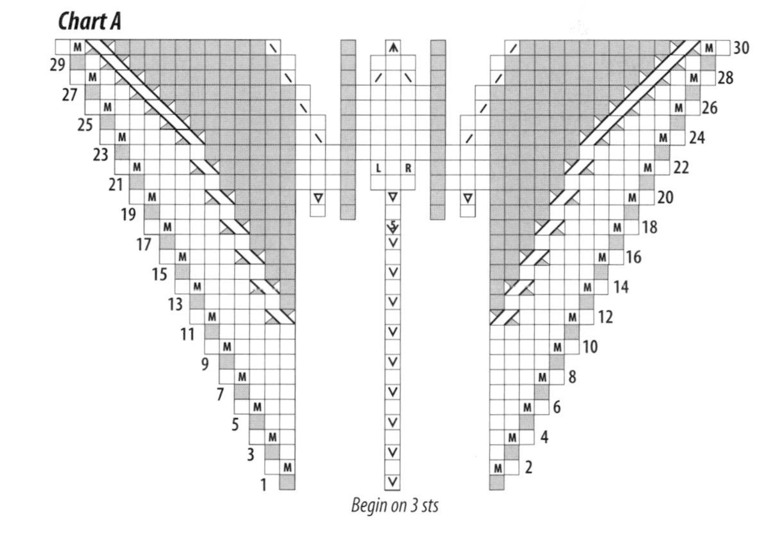

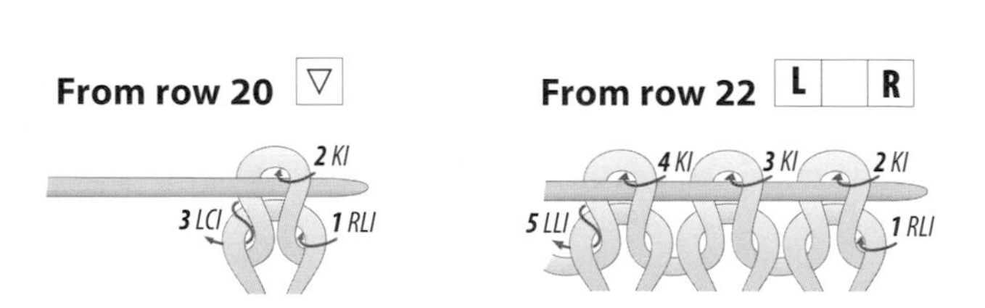

Garter Lace

Designed by
Eugen Beugler

INTERMEDIATE

58" square

10cm/4"

24
over garter stitch (knit every row), blocked

Super fine weight
2700 yds

3.25mm/US 3, or size to obtain gauge, 60cm/24" long or longer

3.5mm/E

&

blocking pins

JAMIESON AND SMITH Shetland Laceweight (100% wool; .88oz/25g; 185yd/170m) in Beige

Note

See *School*, page 102, for yo, SSK, k1 tbl, SK2P, single crochet (sc), and crochet chain (ch)

Blanket

Cast on 3 stitches. ***Next row*** Yo, knit across. Repeat last row until 43 stitches are on needle.

Work charts on page 54 following Blanket Diagram.

After Chart D, each row is worked yo, k3tog, knit to the end. When only 2 stitches remain, k2tog. Fasten off.

Finishing

Crocheted edge

With RS facing and crochet hook, begin at corner and work as follows: * sc, ch1 in each yo loop to corner. In corner loop, (sc, ch1) 3 times. Repeat from *.

Leaving all the ends darned in but not cut off, block the shawl to 58" square. When dry, cut the ends.

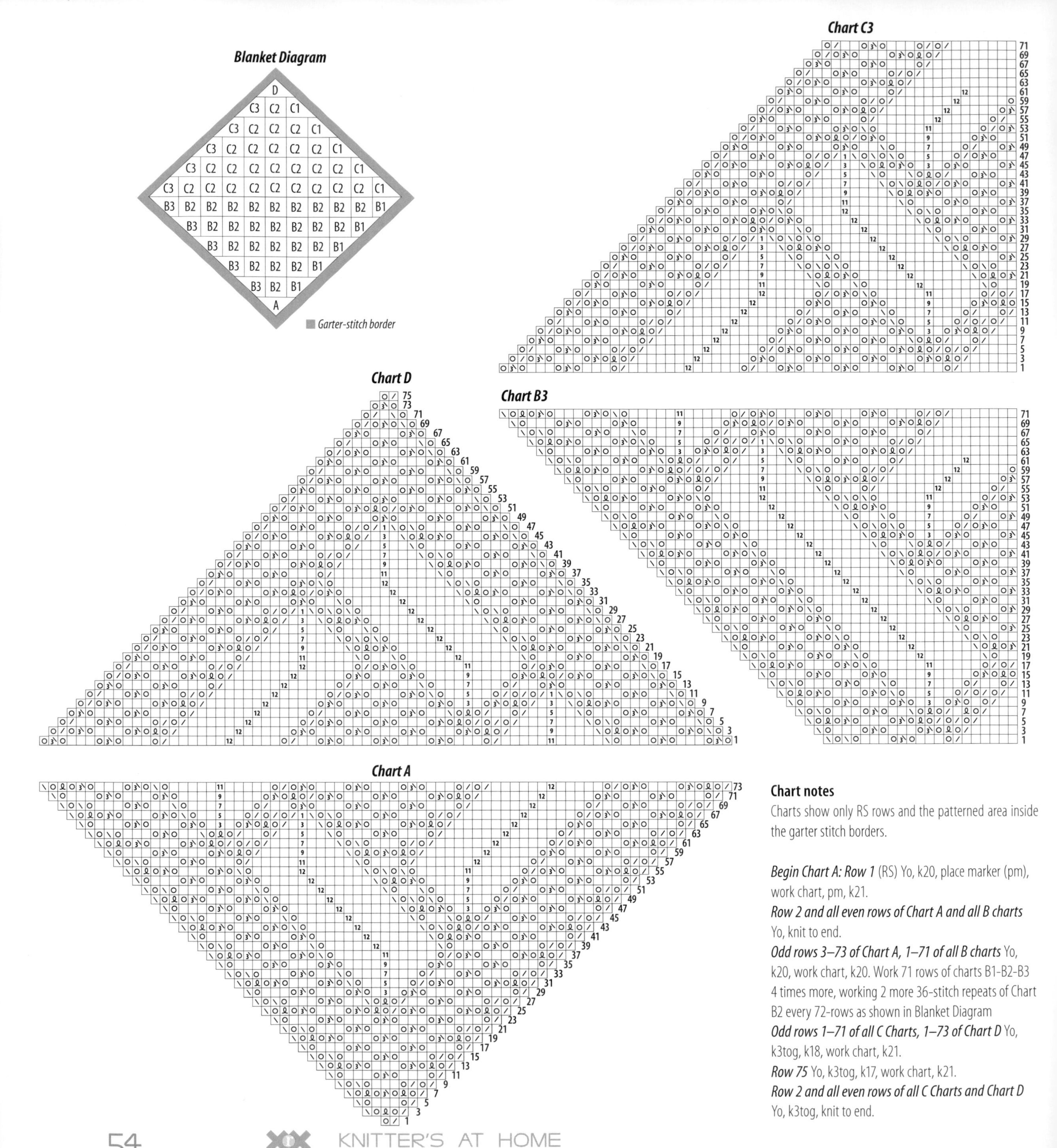

Chart notes

Charts show only RS rows and the patterned area inside the garter stitch borders.

Begin Chart A: Row 1 (RS) Yo, k20, place marker (pm), work chart, pm, k21.

Row 2 and all even rows of Chart A and all B charts Yo, knit to end.

Odd rows 3–73 of Chart A, 1–71 of all B charts Yo, k20, work chart, k20. Work 71 rows of charts B1-B2-B3 4 times more, working 2 more 36-stitch repeats of Chart B2 every 72-rows as shown in Blanket Diagram

Odd rows 1–71 of all C Charts, 1–73 of Chart D Yo, k3tog, k18, work chart, k21.

Row 75 Yo, k3tog, k17, work chart, k21.

Row 2 and all even rows of all C Charts and Chart D Yo, k3tog, knit to end.

Chart C2

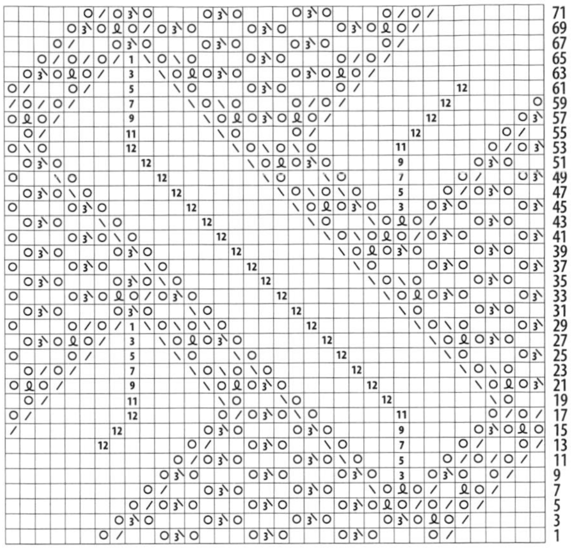

Chart C1

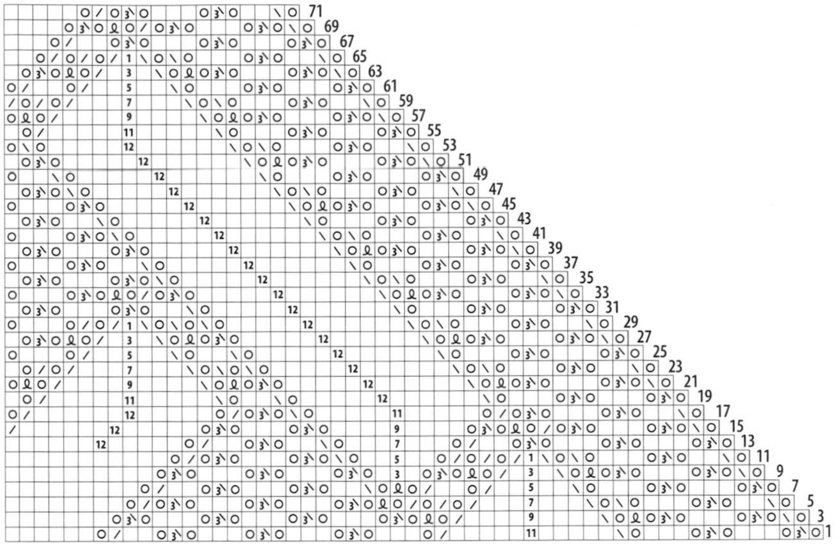

Chart B2

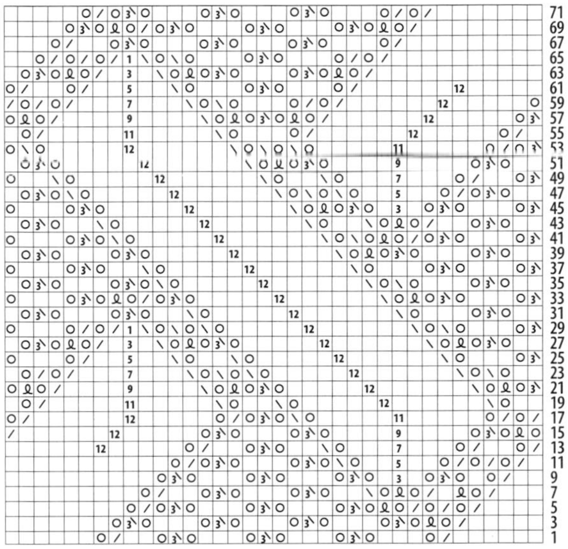

Chart B1

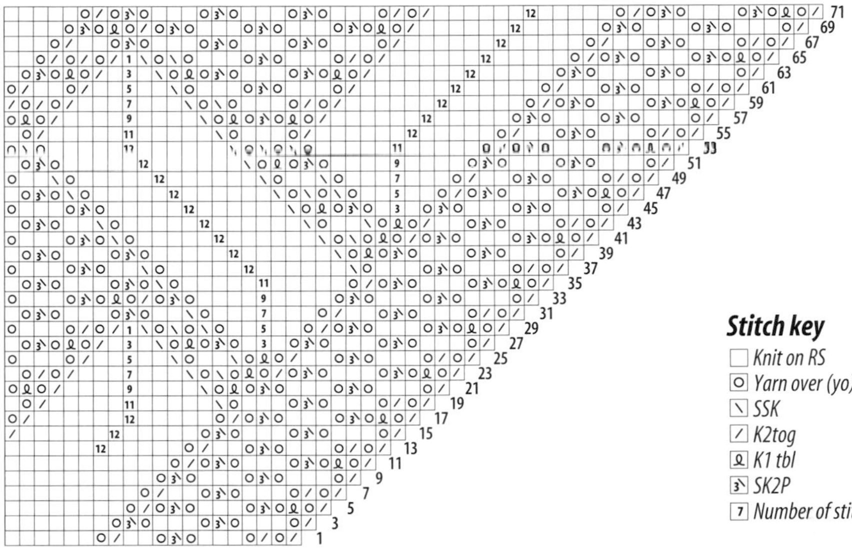

Stitch key

- ☐ Knit on RS
- O Yarn over (yo)
- \ SSK
- / K2tog
- K1 tbl
- SK2P
- 7 Number of stitches to knit

Ribbles Afghan

Designed by
Lily Chin

INTERMEDIATE+

42" × 64"

12cm/4½"

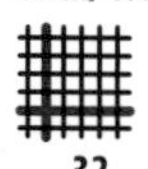

32
over Chart Pattern using larger needle
For gauge swatch, cast on 32 stitches and work chart A, B, or C.

Medium weight
2850 yds

5mm/US 8 and 6mm/US 10, or size to obtain gauge, 74cm (29") long

- stitch markers
- cable needle (cn)

Renaissance Yarns Mohair Mêlé (70% wool, 30% kid mohair; 1¾oz/50g; 150yd/137m) in 4034 Red Earth

Note

Slip stitches purlwise with yarn in back.

Rib Pattern

Row 1 Slip 1, k3, * k1, p1; repeat from * to last 4 stitches, end k4.
Repeat Row 1 for Rib Pattern.

Afghan

With smaller needle, cast on 296 stitches. Work in Rib Pattern for 1", end with a WS row. Change to larger needles. ***Begin Chart Patterns: Row 1*** (RS) Slip 1, k3, place marker (pm), work 32 stitches of Chart A twice, pm, 32 stitches of Chart B 5 times, pm, 32 stitches of Chart C twice, pm, k4. ***Row 2*** Slip 1, k3, work 32 stitches of Chart C twice, 32 stitches of Chart B 5 times, 32 stitches of Chart A twice, k4. Continue in patterns as established until piece measures approximately 63" from beginning. Change to smaller needle. Work in Rib Pattern for 1", end with a WS row. Bind off.

Finishing

Block piece.

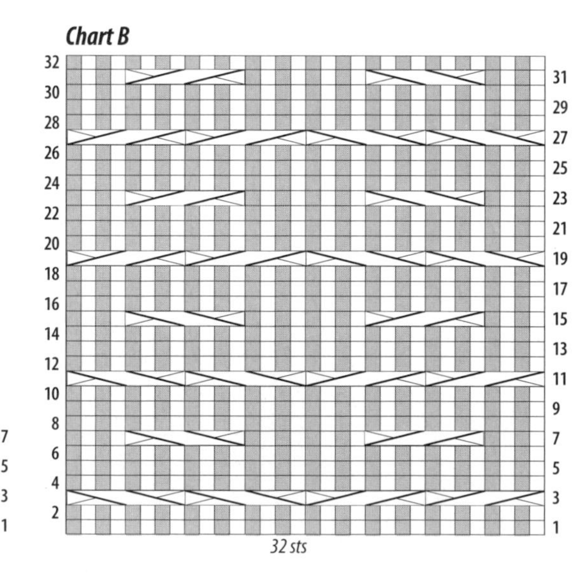

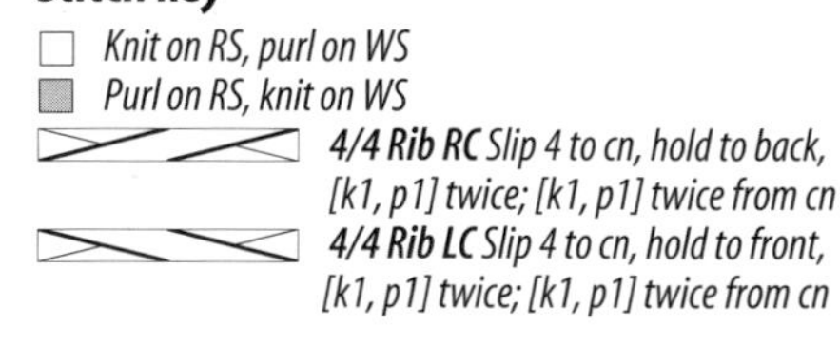

Chart C

32 sts

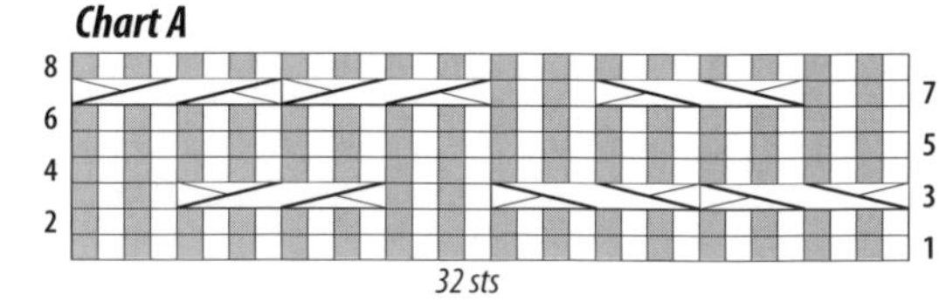

Cables on the Double

Designed by
Lily Chin

INTERMEDIATE

42½" × 54" Blocked

9.52cm/3¾" ***12.7cm/5"***

24

18

over Charts for Side A and B
For gauge swatch, cast on 41 stitches.

1 2 3 **4** 5 6

Medium weight
1767 yds

6.5mm/US 10½", or size to obtain gauge, 60cm/24" or longer

two cable needles (cn)

BERROCO Mohair Classic (78% mohair, 13% wool, 9% nylon; 1½oz/43g; 93yd/85m) in 7912 Quartz

Notes

1 Treat all chart rows as RS rows and read from right to left. **2** Each chart represents one side of the piece, Side A or Side B. When working piece, alternate between Chart for Side A and Chart for Side B every row.

AFGHAN

Cast on 203 stitches. ***Begin Chart for Side A: Row 1*** Sl 1, p1, * k1, p2; repeat from * to end. Turn work. ***Begin Chart for Side B: Row 1*** Sl 1, k1, p1, k2, * p1, k2, p1, 2/1/2 LPC, p1, k2, p1, 2/1/2 RPC; repeat from * to last 18 stitches, p1, k2, p1, 2/1/2 LPC, [p1, k2] 3 times. Turn work. ***Chart for Side A: Row 2*** Repeat row 1 of Chart for Side A. Turn work. ***Chart for Side B: Row 2*** Sl 1, k1, * p1, k2; repeat from * to end. Turn work. Continue in chart patterns as established until 24 rows of Chart B have been worked 5 times, then work rows 1–10 once more (and 6 rows of Chart A have been worked 21 times, then work rows 1–4 once more). Piece measures approximately 54" from beginning. On next row, bind off in pattern (row 5 of Chart for Side A) very tightly.

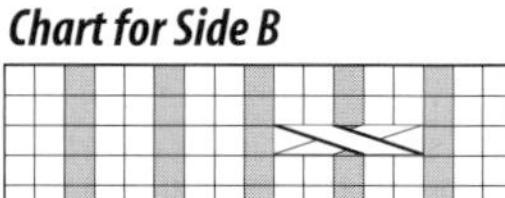

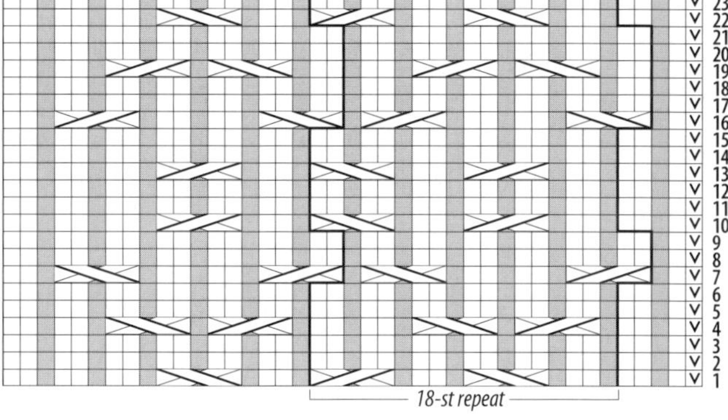

1/2/1 RPC Slip 1 knit stitch and 2 purl stitches to cn and hold to back, k1; slip the 2 purl stitches to left needle, bring cn with knit stitch in front of and to the left of the purl stitches; p2 from left needle; k1 from cn.

1/2/1 LPC Slip 1 knit stitch to cn and hold to front, slip next 2 purl stitches onto a 2nd cn and hold to back, knit next knit stitch; purl 2 from back cn; k1 from front cn.

2/1/2 RPC Slip 2 knit stitches and 1 purl stitch to cn and hold to back, knit next 2 stitches; slip the purl stitch back onto left needle, bring cn with 2 knit stitches in front of and to the left of the purl stitch; p1 from left needle; k2 from cn.

2/1/2 LPC Slip 2 knit stitches to cn and hold to front, slip next purl stitch onto a 2nd cn and hold to back, knit next 2 knit stitches; p1 from back cn; k2 from front cn.

Stitch key
Knit
Purl
Slip 1 purlwise with yarn in front
Slip 1 knitwise with yarn in back
1/2/1 RPC
1/2/1 LPC
2/1/2 RPC
2/1/2 LPC

Ribbles and **Cables on the Double** are reversible cable afghans: both sides of the fabric feature cables, and both sides look good.

Standard cable patterns are worked with stockinette (knit) stitches on a reverse stockinette (purl) stitch base. Reversible cables are worked in ribbed fabrics. Since ribbing is reversible, the cables are too.

Lily Chin developed a family of reversible cables; these afghans are two fine examples. In **Ribbles**, 4 stitches of 1 × 1 rib cross over (or under) another 4 stitches of 1 × 1 rib for a truly reversible cable—both sides of the fabric are the same. **Cables on the Double** is a bit more complicated—a 1 × 2 rib with 2 × 2 cable crossings on one side, and 1 × 1 cable crossings on the other. The secret here is each 2 × 2 cable crosses over a single purl stitch on one side of the fabric, and each 1 × 1 cable crosses over a pair of purl stitches on the opposing side (see illustration).

Lily figured this out and did all the hard work for you. Work a reversible cable swatch; discover how easy it is.

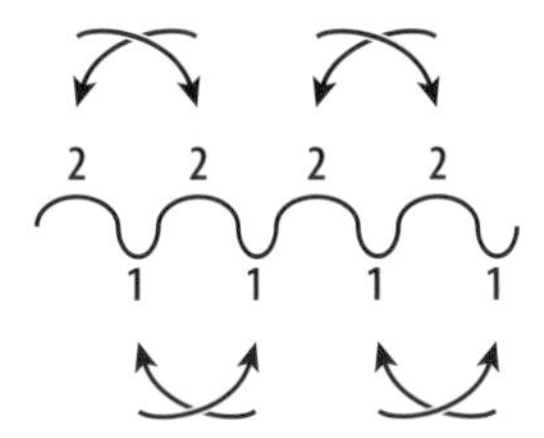

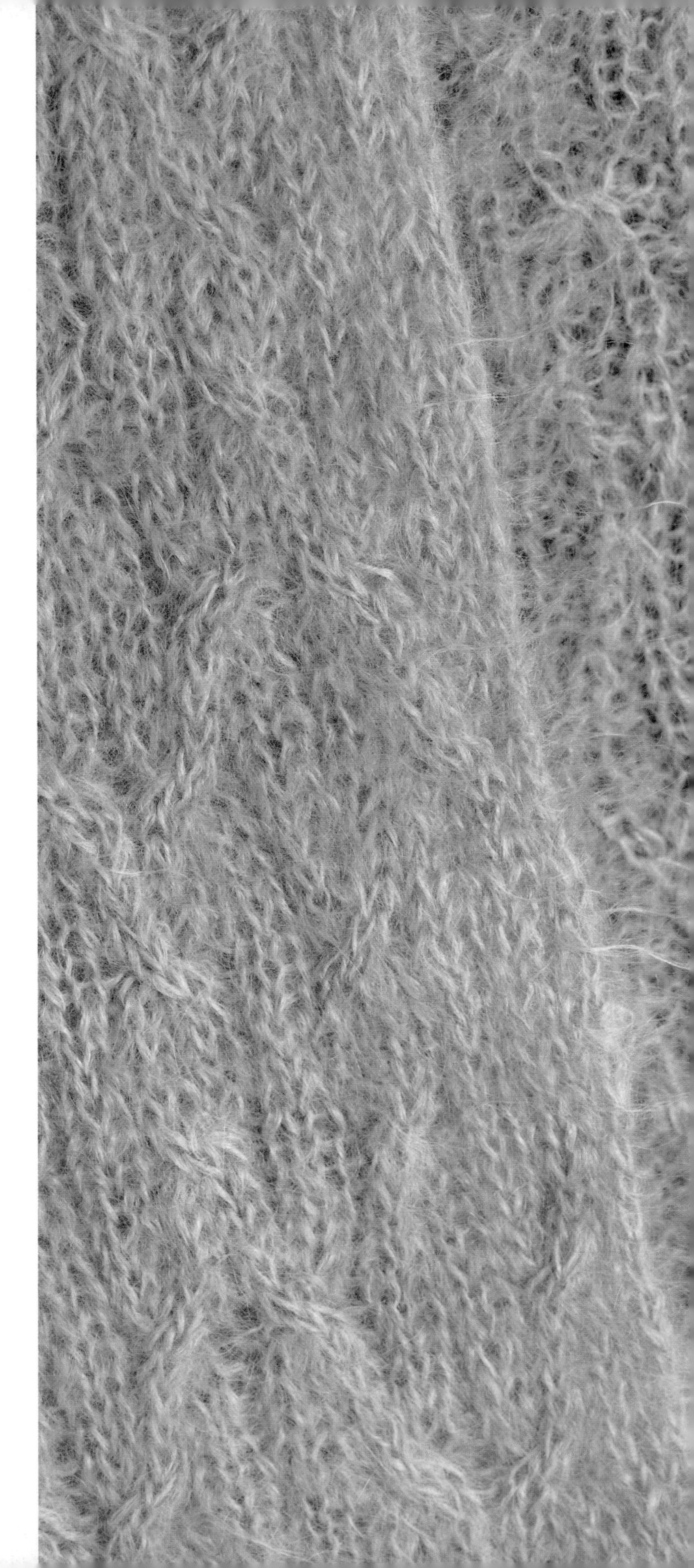

Wraps & Buttons

Designed by
Jill Wolcott

INTERMEDIATE

Approximately 16" × 16"

10cm/4"

16

12

stockinette stitch (knit on RS, purl on WS), after blocking

1 2 3 4 **5** 6

Bulky weight
430 yds

6.5mm/ US 10½, or size to obtain gauge

• tapestry needle
• cable needle (cn)
• 16" square pillow form

CLECKHEATON Tempo (40% acrylic, 30% mohair, 30% wool; 3½oz/100g; 86yd/79m) 1759 Heather

Notes

1 See *School*, page 102, for p1 tbl, and backstitch. **2** Pillow is worked in one piece from back to front.

WRAPPED RIB PILLOW

Cast on 50 stitches. ***Begin Wrapped Rib Chart*** Work rows 1–28 twice, then rows 1–6 once more. Piece measures approximately 16" from beginning.

Work turning ridge: Next row (RS) K2, p24, wrap 10, p24, k2.

Work chart rows 8–28, then rows 1–28, then rows 1–13 once more. Knit 1 row. Piece measures approximately 16" from turning ridge. Bind off all stitches.

Finishing

Block piece. Fold pillow and seam bound-off edge to cast-on edge. Sew one side. Make Tassels and complete pillow (see page 65).

Wrapped Rib Chart

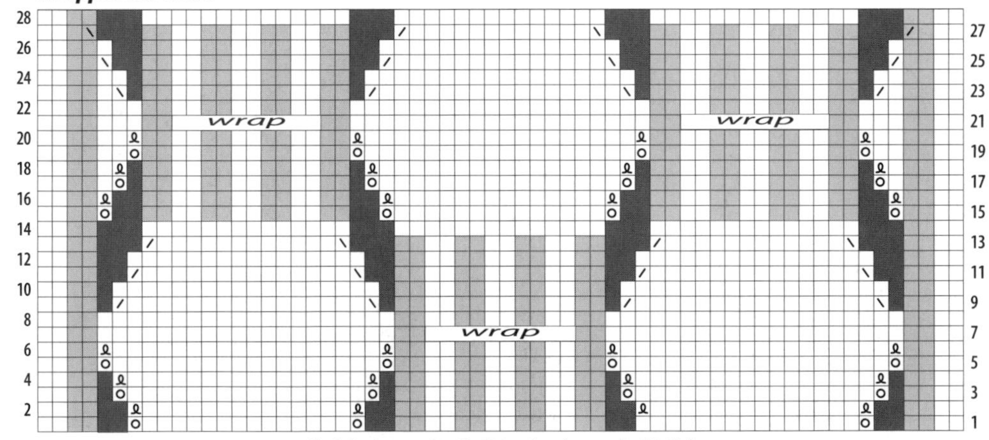

50 stitches increased to 62 stitches then decreased to 50 stitches

Stitch key

- *Knit on RS, purl on WS*
- *Purl on RS, knit on WS*
- *Yarn over*
- *P1 tbl*
- *K2tog*
- *SSK*
- *P2tog*
- *P2tog tbl*
- *Stitches do not exist in these areas of chart*
- wrap: ***Wrap 10*** *Slip 10 stitches to cn, wrap yarn counterclockwise 4 times around stitches (end with yarn on left), slip stitches to right needle*

EASY +

16" × 16"

10cm/4"

28

20
in Block Chart, after blocking

1 2 3 4 5 6

Medium weight
690 yards
small amount of contrast color (CC)

3.75mm/US 5,
or size to obtain gauge

Three 1"/25mm

• tapestry needle
• 16" square pillow form

PATONS Berber Cotton (100% cotton; 3½oz/100g; 230yd/210m) in 3004 multi tweed

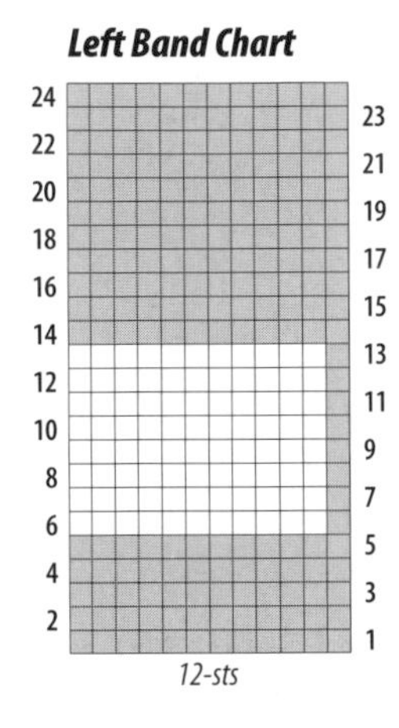

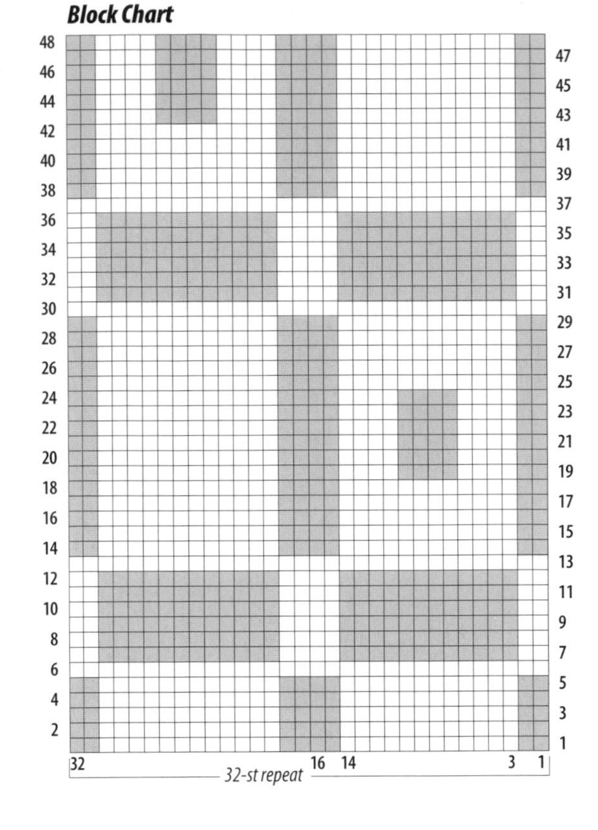

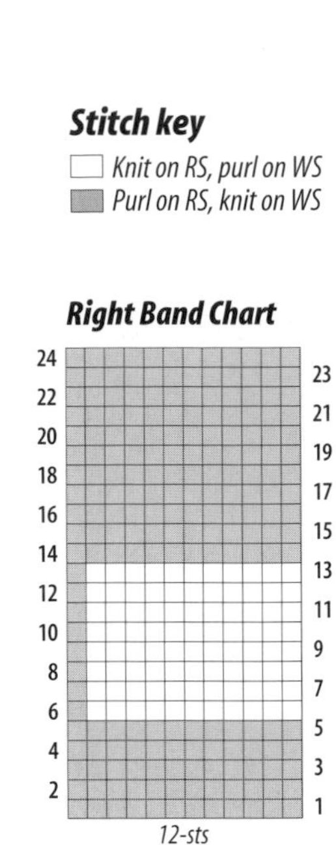

Note

See *School*, page 102, for SSK.

BUTTON PILLOW

Back

Cast on 82 stitches. ***Begin Block Chart: Row 1*** (RS) Knit 1 (selvage), work 32-stitch repeat of Block Chart twice, then work stitches 1–16, end knit 1 (selvage). Keeping first and last stitch in stockinette stitch (knit on RS, purl on WS) as selvage, work chart pattern as established until piece measures 16" from beginning, end with chart row 18. Bind off all stitches.

Right front

Cast on 60 stitches. ***Begin charts: Row 1*** (RS) Knit 1 (selvage), work 12 stitches of Right Band Chart. Work stitches 3–32 of Block Chart, then stitches 1–16, end knit 1 (selvage). Continue in chart patterns as established until piece measures 16" from beginning. Bind off all stitches.

Left front

(**Note** Work buttonhole row as follows: On a WS row, work 3 stitches in pattern, * p4 with (CC) yarn, then return stitches to left needle *, work 13 stitches in pattern (working pattern over CC stitches), repeat from * to * once, work in pattern to end.

Cast on 60 stitches. ***Begin charts: Row 1*** Knit 1 (selvage), work stitches 1–32 of Block Chart, then stitches 1–14. Work 12 stitches of Left Band Chart, end knit 1 (selvage). Continue in chart patterns as established, AT SAME TIME, work buttonholes on row 22 of Block Chart, then on next chart row 10, then chart row 46. When piece measures 16" from beginning, bind off all stitches.

Finishing

Block pieces. Finish each buttonhole as shown. Fold right and left front bands to WS along purl line. Align and stitch buttonholes together. Loosely stitch bands to inside of pillow.

Lap left front over right front and sew 4 sides. Sew on buttons. Insert pillow form.

WORKING THE BUTTONHOLE

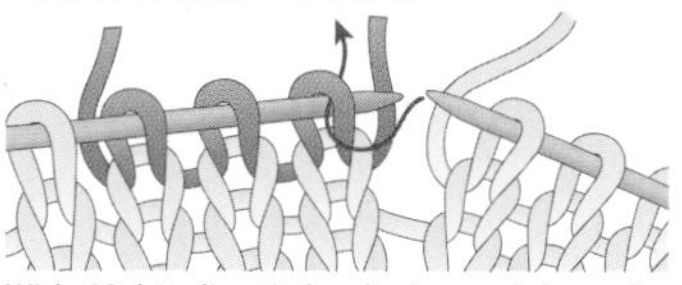

With CC, k3, slip stitches back onto left needle, and continue with MC.

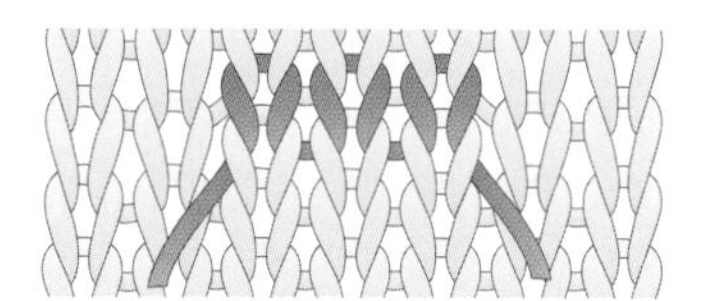

CC marks buttonhole.

FINISHING THE BUTTONHOLE

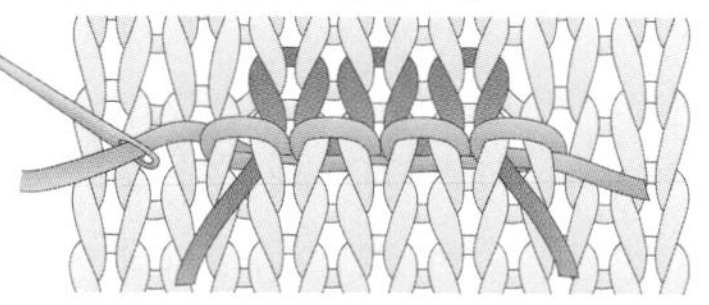

Below CC stitches, backstitch into MC stitches.

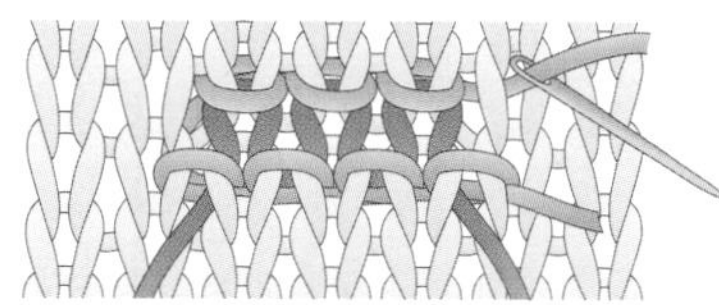

Above CC stitches, backstitch into MC stitches.

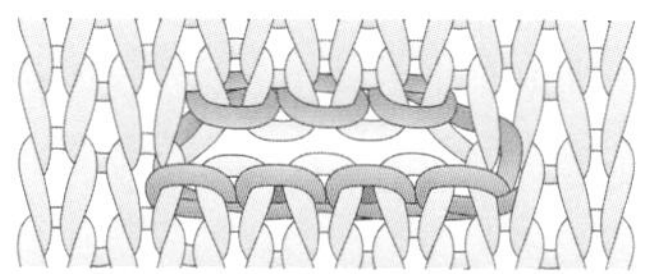

Remove CC and secure ends.

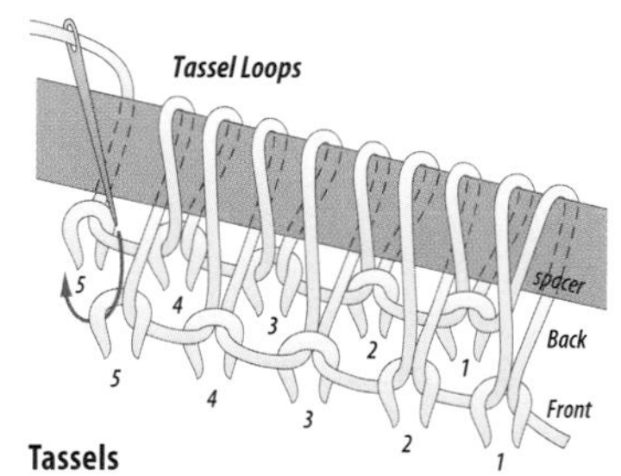

Tassels

With RS facing, pick up and knit 10 stitches diagonally across one corner from edge to edge. ***Next row*** (WS) [P2, k2] twice, p2. Continue in rib pattern as established for 6 rows more. Thread end of yarn through stitches and remove from needle. Repeat ribbing on opposite side of same corner. Do not bind off.

Make tassel loops

Cut a 1½" wide piece of cardboard to use as spacer. Thread a tapestry needle with yarn. With RS facing, thread yarn through Front Stitch 1 from inside to outside, then yarn over spacer from back to front to make 1½" loop, then through Back Stitch 1 from inside to outside, yarn over spacer and through Front Stitch 1 from outside to inside. Continue to weave yarn through stitches (follow diagram) in k2, p2 rib, making loops between stitches, until all stitches have been woven through. Leave a long tail and wrap tail tightly around base of loops. Secure and fasten off.

Work tassels and loops over remaining 3 corners. Insert 16" square pillow form through opening. Sew opening together.

The Cozy Generation

Designed by
Traci Bunkers

INTERMEDIATE

42" × 60" (excluding fringe)

10cm/4"

16

11
over Chart Pattern

Medium weight
A & B • 1576 yds each

8mm/US 11, or size to obtain gauge, 90cm/36" long

6mm/J

• cable needle (cn)
• stitch markers

LION BRAND Wool Ease (80% acrylic, 20% wool; 3oz/85g; 197yds/177m) in 130 Green Heather (A), 131 Green Sprinkles (B)

Notes

1 See *School*, page 102, for kf&b, SK2P, and attaching fringe. **2** Afghan is worked back and forth in rows on a circular needle. **3** Use 2 strands of yarn held together throughout.

Border Pattern (Over an odd number of stitches)
Row 1 (RS) * K1, p1; repeat from *, end k1.
Row 2 Knit.
Repeat rows 1–2 for Border Pattern.

Afghan

With 1 strand each A and B held together, loosely cast on 113 stitches. Work 5 rows in Border Pattern. ***Next (increase) row*** (WS) K8, * kf&b next stitch, k31; repeat from * twice more, kf&b, k8—117 stitches. ***Work in Chart Pattern*** until piece measures 58½" from beginning, end with a WS row. Work 6 rows in Border Pattern, decreasing 1 stitch over each 8-stitch cable (by k2tog) on first row—113 stitches. Bind off all stitches loosely.

Finishing

Lightly block piece.

Fringe

With both yarns held together, cut 18" pieces of yarn. With 4 strands of each color held together, attach fringe with crochet hook every 4 or 5 stitches along short sides.

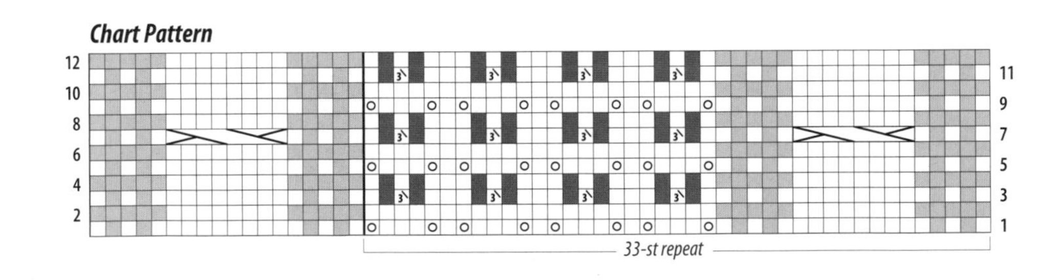

Stitch key

Knit on RS, purl on WS
Purl on RS, knit on WS
SK2P
Yarn over
4/4 LC
Slip 4 to cn and hold to front, k4; k4 from cn
Stitches do not exist in these areas of chart

Shaker Throw

Designed by
Dott Grubbs

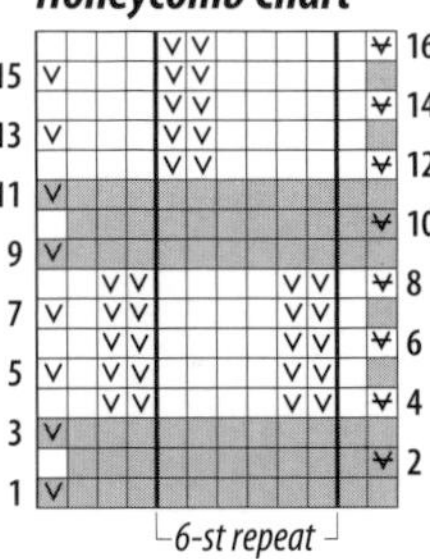

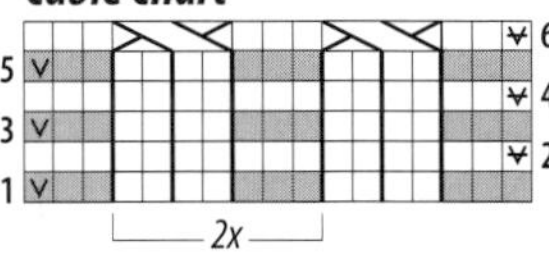

INTERMEDIATE

40" × 46" including fringe

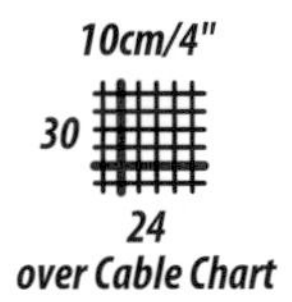

Light weight
2337 yds

3.75mm/US 5, or size to obtain gauge

&

- cable needle (cn)
- tapestry needle

REYNOLDS Saucy Sportweight (100% mercerized cotton; 1¾oz/50g; 123yd/112m) in 809 Ivory

Notes

1 See *School*, page 102, for mattress stitch, SSK, and yo. **2** Slip all first stitches purlwise with yarn in front unless otherwise instructed.

Honeycomb squares *(Make 9)*

Cast on 54 stitches. [Work rows 1–16 of Honeycomb Chart] 6 times. Repeat Rows 1–3. Bind off, leaving a 12" tail for sewing.

Cable strips *(Make 12 strips of 8" and 4 strips of 40")*

Cast on 24 stitches. Work rows 1–6 of Cable Chart for 8(40)". Repeat rows 1–3. Bind off, leaving a tail for sewing.

Edging & fringe *(Make 2 strips)*

The fringe is added to the edging as it is knitted. Cut 7" strands, 100 at a time.
Cast on 18 stitches. ***Row 1*** Slip 1, k1, yo, SSK, k9, yo, SSK, place 2 strands of fringe over working yarn and fold to double, purl 3. ***Row 2*** Place the 4 ends of fringe over working yarn, purl 3 stitches locking the fringe in place, k1, yo, SSK, knit the next 8 stitches wrapping yarn around needle 4 times for each stitch (elongated stitches, see figure 1), k1, yo, SSK, k1. ***Row 3*** Slip 1, k1, yo, SSK, slip next 8 stitches onto right needle dropping the extra wraps as the stitches are moved. The 8 slipped stitches are now on right needle (see figure 2); pass left needle through stitches 4, 3, 2, 1 and pull them over stitches 5, 6, 7, 8. Slip all stitches back to left needle (see figure 3), then knit them in their new order; k1, yo, SSK, add fringe as in row 1, purl 3. ***Row 4*** Lock fringe as in row 2, purling 3 stitches; k1, yo, SSK, k1, yo, SSK, k1. Repeat rows 1–4 for 40".

Finishing

Make pieces and join using matress stitch and folowing Joining Diagram.

Stitch key

- *Knit on RS, purl on WS*
- *Purl on RS, knit on WS*
- *Slip 1 with yarn on WS of work*
- *Slip 1 with yarn on RS of work*
- ***2/2 LC*** *Slip 2 to cn, hold in front, k2; k2 from cn*

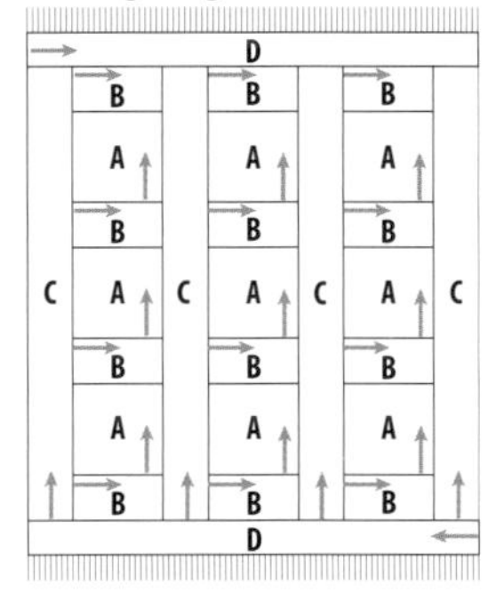

A Honeycomb squares
B Short cable strips
C Long cable strips
D Fringed Edging

Elongated stitch

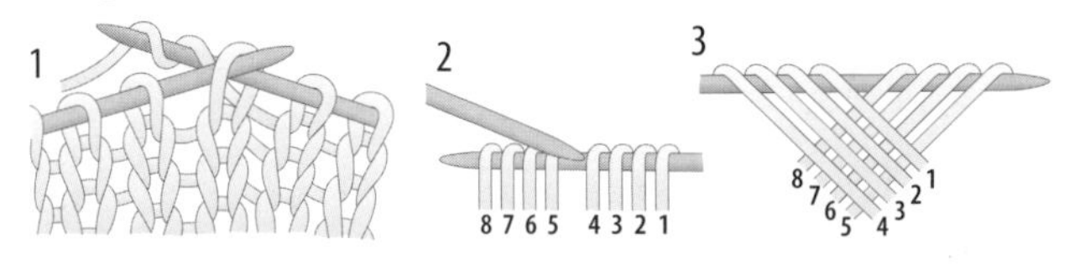

To elongate a stitch, wrap yarn around needle more than one time. The afghan's edging uses stitches wrapped four times around needle. On the following row, the extra wraps are dropped as the stitches are slipped to the right needle (figure 2), then crossed (figure 3) before knitting in the new order.

A Round Aran

Designed by
Diane Zangl

INTERMEDIATE

18" × 9"

10cm/4"

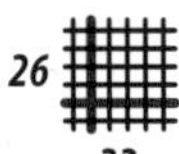

over stockinette stitch (knit every round) using smaller needle

Medium weight
591 yds each pillow

• 4mm/US 6, or size to obtain gauge, 40cm/16" long
• 4.5mm/US 7, 60cm/24" long

Four 4mm/US 6

• cable needle (cn)
• stitch markers
• bolster pillow form

LION BRAND Wool Ease (80% acrylic, 20% wool; 3oz/85g; 197yd/180m) in 99 Fisherman, 107 Blue Heather

Notes

1 See *School*, page 102, for S2KP2, attached I-cord, and grafting. **2** Change to double-pointed needles (dpn) when necessary.

WHITE VERSION

End pieces *(Make 2)*

With smaller needle, cast on 150 stitches. Place marker (pm) and join, being careful not to twist stitches. ***Rounds 1, 3, 5, 7, 9, 11, 13, 14, 16, 17, 19, 20, 22, 23, 25, 26, 28, 29*** Knit. ***Round 2*** * K11, S2KP2, k11; repeat from *. ***Round 4*** * K10, S2KP2, k10; repeat from *. ***Round 6*** * K9, S2KP2, k9; repeat from *. ***Round 8*** * K8, S2KP2, k8; repeat from *. ***Round 10*** * K7, S2KP2, k7; repeat from *. ***Round 12*** * K6, S2KP2, k6; repeat from *. ***Round 15*** * K5, S2KP2, k5; repeat from *. ***Round 18*** * K4, S2KP2, k4; repeat from *. ***Round 21*** * K3, S2KP2, k3; repeat from *. ***Round 24*** * K2, S2KP2, k2; repeat from *. ***Round 27*** * K1, S2KP2, k1; repeat from *. ***Round 30*** [S2KP2] 6 times—6 stitches. Cut yarn, draw through remaining stitches and secure to inside. With dpn, work 3-stitch attached I-cord around edge, picking up 1 stitch in each cast-on stitch. Graft open stitches to cast-on stitches.

Body

With RS of one end-piece facing and larger needle, pick up and knit 150 stitches along inside stitches of I-cord (closest to end piece). Pm and work in rounds as follows: ***Begin Charts A and B: Round 1*** [Work 8 stitches Chart A, 17 stitches Chart B] 6 times. Continue in pattern as established until 22 rounds of Chart B have been worked 5 times. Work 3 more rounds, binding off in pattern on last round.

Finishing

Insert pillow form. Graft bound-off stitches of body to inside stitches of I-cord of remaining end-piece.

BLUE VERSION

Work as for White Version, except work Charts C and D.

Chart B

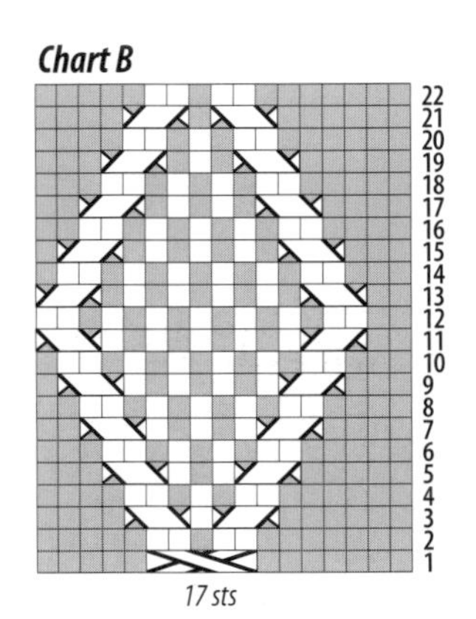

17 sts

Chart A

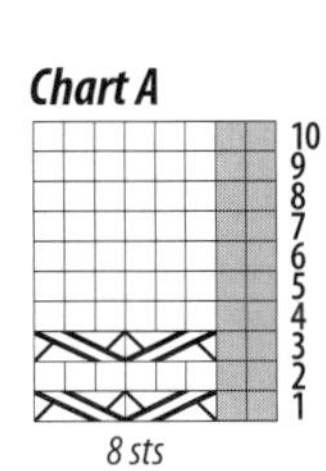

8 sts

Chart D

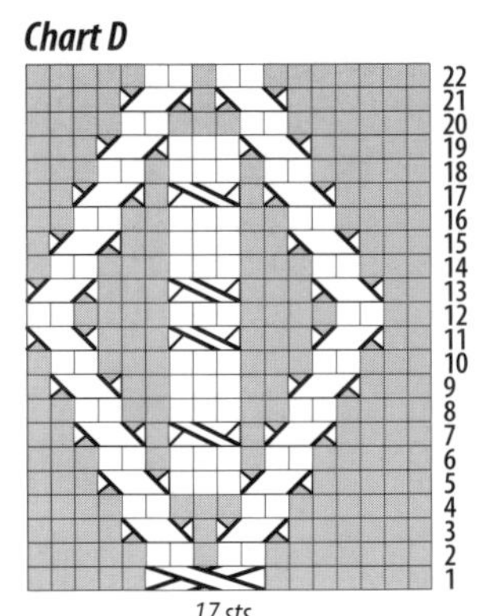

17 sts

Chart C

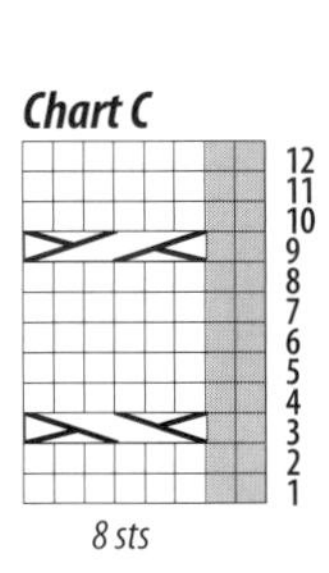

8 sts

Stitch key

Knit
Purl
1/2 RC *Slip 2 to cn, hold to back, k1; k2 from cn*
1/2 LC *Slip 1 to cn, hold to front, k2; k1 from cn*
2/1 RPC *Slip 1 to cn, hold to back, k2; p1 from cn*
2/1 LPC *Slip 2 to cn, hold to front, p1; k2 from cn*
2/1/2 LPC *Slip 3 to cn, hold to front, k2; sl last stitch from cn to left needle and p it; k2 from cn*
3/3 RC *Slip 3 to cn, hold to back, k3; k3 from cn*
3/3 LC *Slip 3 to cn, hold to front, k3; k3 from cn*

Thick Woven Blanket

Designed by
Elena Malo

EASY +

55" square

10cm/4"

24

11

over Woven Pattern

Medium weight
A • 1950 yds
B • 910 yds
C • 130 yds

10mm/US 15 and 12.75mm/US 17, or size to obtain gauge, 80cm/32" long or longer

tapestry needle

BERNAT Misti (50% acrylic, 35% mohair, 15% wool; 1¾oz/50g; 130yd/118m) in White (A), Ashes of Roses (B), Lavender (C)

Notes

1 See *School*, page 102, for kf&b. **2** Slip all stitches as if to purl and with yarn on WS. **3** Work with 2 strands held together throughout project. **4** Carry yarns loosely along side edge.

Blanket

With 2 strands of B and larger needles, cast on 123 stitches. ***Row 1*** (WS) With B, knit. ***Rows 2 and 3*** With A, knit. ***Row 4*** With B, knit. ***Row 5*** With B, purl. Work Woven Pattern chart until piece measaures 46" from beginning, end with chart row 4. With B, knit 1 row, purl 1 row. With A, knit 2 rows. With B, knit 2 rows. Do not bind off.

Border

With A and smaller needles, continue on 123 stitches as follows:
RS rows Kf&b, knit to last stitch, kf&b—2 stitches increased.
WS rows Knit. Repeat last 2 rows for 5". Bind off on WS.
Work border on 3 remaining sides of blanket, picking up 125 stitches on first row. Sew border at each corner.

Weaving

Weave doubled strands of C under A stitches and over B stitches every 4th row of Woven Pattern.

Woven Pattern

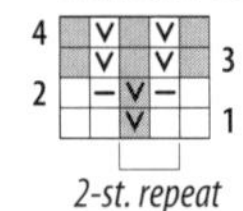

2-st. repeat

Stitch key

- *Knit on RS, purl on WS*
- *Purl on RS, knit on WS*
- *Slip 1 with yarn on WS*

Color key

- *A*
- *B*

For the Home

Designed by
Sue Mink

EASY

42" × 68" excluding fringe

10cm/4"

9 [gauge grid] 8

in Pattern Stitch, using 1 strand each A, B, C held together

1 2 3 4 **5** 6

Bulky weight
A • 1155 yds

1 2 3 **4** 5 6

Medium weight
B • 930 yds
C • 1080 yds

10mm/US 15, or size to obtain gauge

6.5mm/K

ORIGINAL YARN

BERROCO Chinchilla (100% rayon; 1¾oz/50g; 77yd/70m) in 5103 Taupe (A); Mohair Classic (78% mohair, 13% wool, 9% nylon; 1½oz/40g; 93yd/85m) in 9538 Taupe (B); Europa (75% superwash wool, 25% cotton; 1¾oz/50g; 135yd/121m) in 1207 Aztec (C)

Notes

1 See *School*, page 102, for attaching fringe. **2** Use 3 strands of yarn held together throughout.

Pattern Stitch *(over an odd number of stitches)*

Row 1 (RS) Knit.
Row 2 * P1, k1; repeat from *, end p1.
Repeat rows 1 and 2 for Pattern Stitch.

Throw

With 1 strand each of A, B, and C held together, cast on 83 stitches. Work in Pattern Stitch for 68". Bind off loosely in pattern.

Finishing

Block piece.

Fringe

Holding 1 strand of each yarn together, cut 16" lengths. Work fringe along top and lower edges. Trim the fringe.

What is simpler than a big needle knit? This quick, multi-strand afghan is comfort knitting. The stitch is broken rib: one row of 1×1 rib alternates with one knit row. The yarns can be any combination, but be sure to include a mohair strand. No need to match the gauge; cast on an odd number of stitches that gives you the size afghan you want and enjoy.

Soft Geometry

Adobe Bricks

Designed by
Barbara Venishnick

Chart Pattern

7-st repeat

14-row repeat

Stitch key

Knit on RS, purl on WS

Purl on RS, knit on WS

Slip 1 purlwise with yarn at WS of work

Color key

MC

CC

EASY +

Afghan 36" × 50"
Pillow 14" × 14"

10cm/4"

26/28

19/21
over Chart Pattern, using 6mm/US 10 4mm/US6 needles

1 2 3  5 6

Medium weight
MC • 1425 yds
CC • 435 yds
MC • 380 yds
CC • 180 yds

6mm/US 10, or size to obtain gauge
4mm/US 6, or size to obtain gauge

6mm/US 10, 101cm/40" long

14" square pillow form

PLYMOUTH Bella Colour (55% cotton, 45% acrylic; 1¾oz/50g; 104yd/95m) in 13 (MC); P-Zazz (65% nylon, 35% rayon; 1¾oz/50g; 61yd/56m) in 6174 (CC)

AFGHAN

Square *(Make 48)*
With MC, cast on 32 stitches. Work rows 1–4 of Chart Pattern, then work 14-row repeat twice, work rows 19–26 once. Bind off.

Finishing
Block squares. * Following Joining Diagram for square orientation, sew 8 squares together for strip A, and another 8 squares for strip B. Repeat from * twice more. Sew all strips together, alternating A and B strips.
Edging
With RS facing, circular needle and CC, * pick up and knit 180 stitches along one shorter edge of afghan (30 stitches along each square). Knit 1 row on WS. Bind off, leaving last stitch on right needle. Pick up and knit 240 stitches (including stitch on needle) along longer edge. Knit 1 row. Bind off, leaving last stitch on needle. Repeat from * once more. Cut yarn after last bound-off stitch, draw yarn through loop and sew it to first bound-off stitch of first side.

PILLOW

With MC, cast on 60 stitches. Work rows 1–4 of Chart Pattern, then work 14-row repeat 6 times, work rows 19–26 once. Bind off. Repeat for other side.

Finishing
Block pieces. Sew pieces together on 3 edges, insert pillow form, sew remaining edge.

As seen on page 97: NATURALLY HAND KNIT YARNS Vero (100% wool; 1¾oz/50g; 87yd/80m) in 15 (MC); TRENDSETTER YARNS Joy (75% polyamide, 25% polyester; 1oz/25g; 62yd/57m) in 330 Grape Galaxy (A); Dolcino (75% acrylic myolis, 25% polyamide; 1¾oz/50g; 99yd/90m) in 111 Cream (B)

Joining Diagram

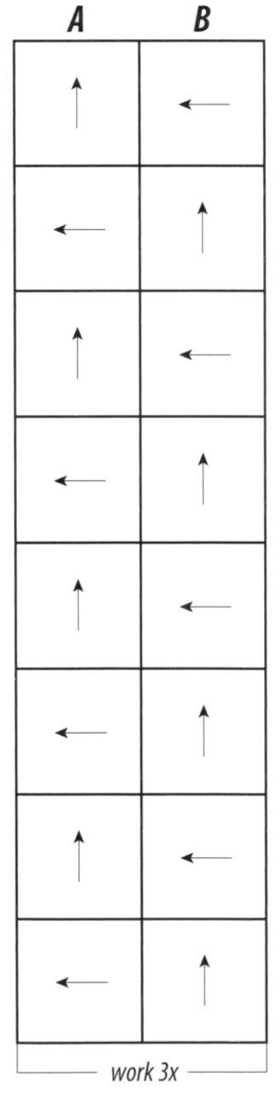

Mesa Verde

Designed by
Kathy Cheifetz

EASY+

Afghan • 34½" × 53"
Pillow • 14" × 14"

10cm/4"

over Pattern Stitch

1 2 3 4 5 6

Bulky weight
Afghan
MC • 550 yds
CC • 340 yds
Pillow
MC • 131 yds
CC • 75 yds

Afghan • 6.5mm/US 10½ or size to obtain gauge, 91cm/36" long

Pillow • 6.5mm/US 10½, or size to obtain gauge

Pillow • Four 38mm (1½")

• stitch markers
• 14" square pillow form

COLINETTE Prism (70% wool, 30% cotton; 3½oz/100g; 131yd/120m) in 113 (MC), 75 (CC)

Note

See *School*, page 102, for SK2P, kf&b, and long-tail cast-on.

Pattern Stitch

Multiple Of 13 Stitches

Row 1 (RS) * Kf&b in next stitch, k4, SK2P, k4, kf&b; repeat from * to end.

Row 2 Purl.

Repeat rows 1 and 2 for Pattern Stitch.

PILLOW FOLDING DIAGRAM

Stripe Pattern

* 12 rows MC, 8 rows CC; repeat from * (20 rows) for Stripe Pattern.

AFGHAN

With MC, cast on 138 stitches. Work Pattern Stitch and Stripe Pattern at the same time as follows: ***Row 1*** (RS) With MC, k4, place marker (pm), work Pattern Stitch to last 4 stitches, pm, k4. Continue in pattern as established, keeping 4 stitches at each side in garter stitch (knit every row), until 20 rows of Stripe Pattern have been worked 10 times, then work rows 1–12 of Stripe Pattern once more. Piece measures approximately 53" from beginning. Bind off.

Finishing

Block piece.

PILLOW

With MC, cast on 54 stitches, using long-tail cast-on. Work Pattern Stitch and Stripe Pattern at the same time as follows: ***Row 1*** (RS) With MC, k1, work Pattern Stitch to last stitch, k1. Continue in pattern as established, keeping 1 stitch at each side in garter stitch (knit every row), until 20 rows of Stripe Pattern have been worked 5 times, then work rows 1–12 of Stripe Pattern once more. Piece measures approximately 30" from beginning. Bind off.

Finishing

Block piece. Fold pillow so that first MC stripe overlaps last MC stripe (see diagram below) and sew cast-on edge of first stripe along first row of last stripe (marked by dotted line), using an overcast seam and MC. Sew one side. Insert pillow form. Sew remaining side. Sew on buttons, using photo as guide.

Try your own colors online at
www.KnittingUniverse.com/PAINTBOX.

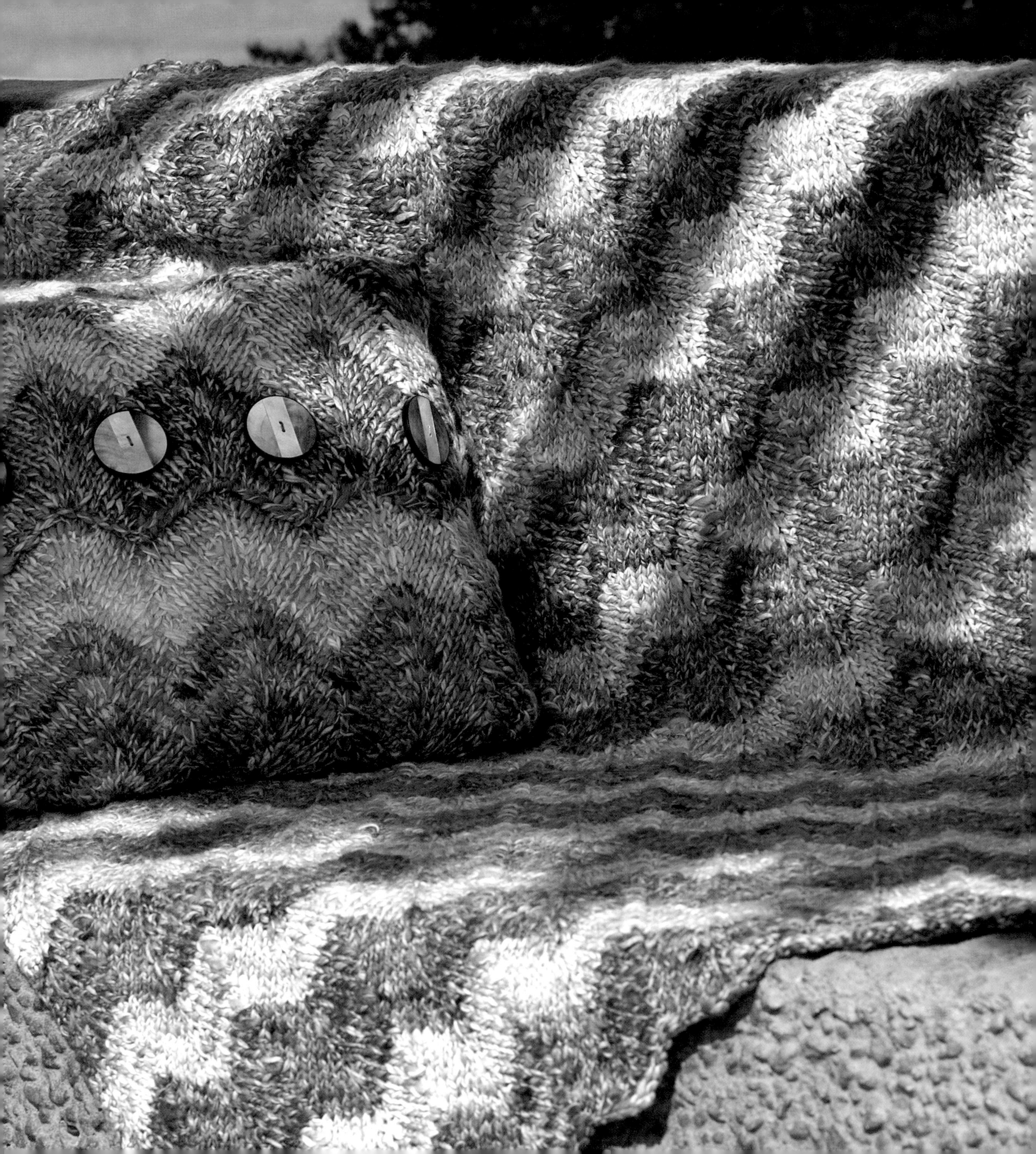

Twill & Kente

Designed by
Barbara Venishnick

INTERMEDIATE

16" × 16"

10cm/4"

26

20
over Chart A

Medium weight
528 yds

4.5mm/US 7, or size to obtain gauge, 60cm/24" long or longer

16" square pillow form

REYNOLDS Eternity (51% wool, 49% microfiber; 1¾oz/50g; 88yd/80m) in 775 Navy

TWILL PILLOW

Front/Back

Cast on 77 stitches. Work 12 rows of Chart A 9 times, then work rows 1 and 2 once more. Bind off. Repeat for other side.

Finishing

Reverse stockinette stitch edging Place pieces with WS together, and bound off and cast-on edges together. Pick up and knit 72 stitches along each of three sides (working through both thicknesses)—216 stitches. * [Knit 1 row, purl 1 row] 3 times. Bind off *. Stretch piece over pillow form. Pick up and knit 72 stitches along remaining side (again working through both layers). Work from * to * once. Sew corners. Allow edging to curl over seam and sew to pillow, covering pick-up row.

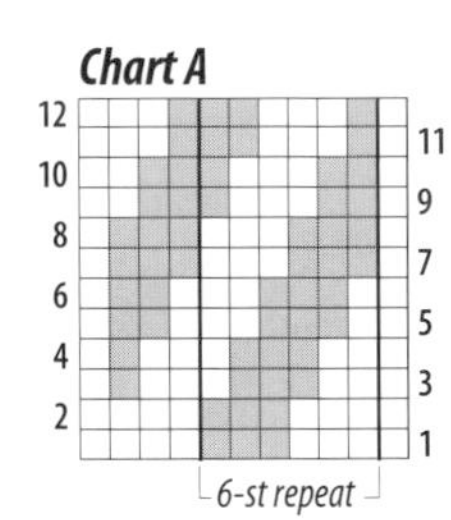

Stitch key
- *Knit on RS, purl on WS*
- *Purl on RS, knit on WS*

INTERMEDIATE

16" × 16"

10cm/4"

40

20
over garter stitch (knit every row)

Medium weight

MC • 352 yards
A • 264 yards
B • 176 yards

4.5mm/US 7, or size to obtain gauge 60cm/24" long or longer

3.75mm/F

16" square pillow form

REYNOLDS Eternity (51% wool, 49% microfiber; 1¾oz/50g; 88yd/80m) 751 Beige (MC), 750 White (A), 775 Navy (B)

Notes

1 See *School*, page 102, for intarsia and single crochet. **2** Slip stitches purlwise with yarn at WS. **3** Front and back are each made in 4 separate vertical strips, which are then crocheted together. **4** Each strip consists of 4 patterns. **5** Bind off after completing each strip.

KENTE PILLOW

Pattern I *(Over 23 stitches and 34 rows)*

Rows 1, 2 With B, knit. ***Rows 3, 4*** With MC, [k1, sl1] 11 times, k1. ***Rows 5, 6*** With B, Knit. ***Rows 7, 8*** With A, [sl 1, k1] 11 times, sl 1. ***Rows 9–32*** Repeat rows 1–8 three times. ***Rows 33, 34*** With B, knit.

Pattern II *(Over 23 stitches and 44 rows)*

Row 1 With B, [sl 1, k1] 11 times, sl 1. ***Row 2*** Sl 1, [p1, sl 1] 11 times. ***Rows 3, 4*** With MC, [k1, sl 1] 11 times, k1. ***Rows 5–44*** Repeat rows 1–4 ten times.

Pattern III *(Over 23 stitches and 34 rows)*

Rows 1, 2 With MC, knit. ***Rows 3, 4*** With B, [k1, sl 1] 11 times, k1. ***Rows 5–32*** Repeat rows 1–4 seven times. ***Rows 33, 34*** With MC, knit.

Pattern IV *(Over 23 stitches and 34 rows)*

Rows 1, 2 With MC, knit. ***Rows 3, 4*** With A, k1, [sl 1, k3] 5 times, sl 1, k1. ***Rows 5, 6*** With MC, k1, [k1, sl 1] 10 times, k2. ***Rows 7, 8*** Repeat rows 3 and 4. ***Rows 9–32*** Repeat rows 1–8 three times. ***Rows 33, 34*** With MC, knit.

Front/Back

Strip 1 With B, cast on 23 stitches. Work Pattern I, Chart B, Pattern II, Chart C ***Strip 2*** With A, cast on 23 stitches. Work Chart C, Pattern III, Chart D, Pattern I ***Strip 3*** With MC, cast on 23 stitches. Work Pattern II, Pattern IV, Pattern I, Chart B. ***Strip 4*** With MC, cast on 23 stitches. Work Chart D (reversing colors), Pattern, Chart C, Pattern III.

Finishing

Following Joining Diagram for placement, join strips as follows: Place WS of Strips 1 and 2 together. With crochet hook and MC, working through both thicknesses, join strips with single crochet in each row, skipping rows occasionally as needed to stay flat. Join Strip 3, then Strip 4 in same way. Repeat for other side. With MC, join front and back and work edging as for Twill pillow.

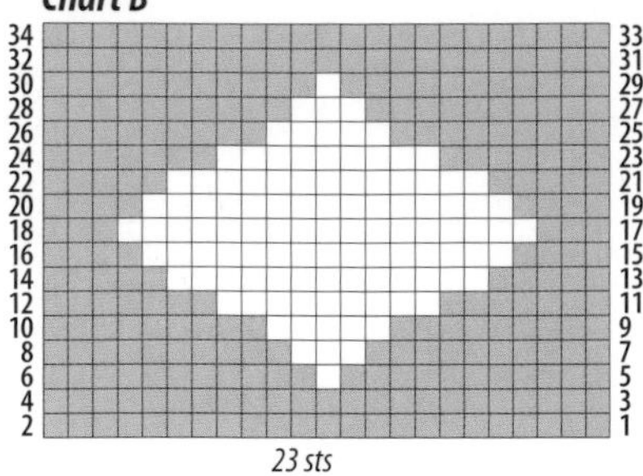

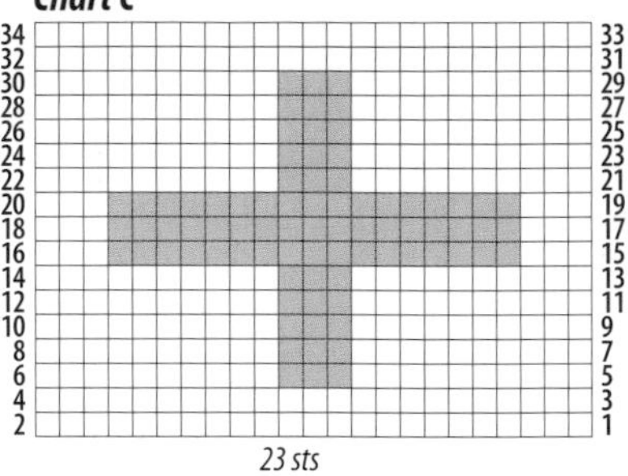

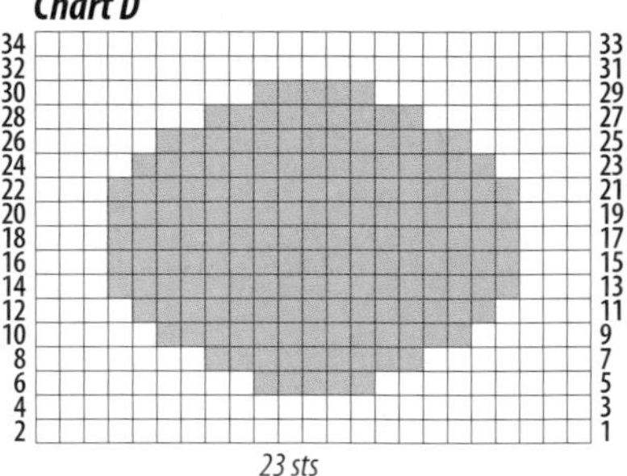

Color key
MC
A

Chart notes

1 *Knit every row.* ***2*** *Work each chart row twice, once on RS, and once on WS.* ***3*** *Use separate strand of yarn for each block of color; at color changes, bring new color under old.*

Next page, Tobin's Tiles, instructions follow.

Tobin's Tiles

Designed by
Michele Maks

INTERMEDIATE

56" × 63" without edging

10cm/4"

25

14
over Swatch Chart

Medium weight
MC • 1350 yds
CC • 1215 yds

6mm/US10, or size to obtain gauge, 80cm/32" long or longer

tapestry needle

Original yarn
BRUNSWICK Windmist (100% acrylic; 1¾oz/50g; 135yd/123m) in 2819 Black (MC), 2847 Norwegian Spruce (CC).

Afghan on following page: UNIVERSAL YARN, INC. Deluxe Chunky (100% wool; 3½oz/100g; 120yd/110m) in 91872 Dusk (MC), 3777 Cobalt (CC), 41759 Nectarine (A), 61633 Greenery (B) Border worked in 1 ridge each as follows: MC, B, MC, A, MC

Heart block on following page: MALABRIGO YARN Chunky (100% superfine merino wool; 3½oz/100g; 104yd/95m) in Vermillion and Tiger Lily

AFGHAN

With MC, cast on 201. Change to CC. ***Begin Diamond Chart: Rows 1 and 2*** K25, p1, [k49, p1] 3 times, k25. Change to MC. ***Rows 3 and 4*** P24, k3, [p47, k3] 3 times, p24. Continue working from Diamond Chart, changing colors every 2 rows, for a total of 4 repeats of Diamond Chart. Work rows 1 and 2 of chart. Do not bind off. ***Top border: Row 1*** (RS) Knit. ***Row 2*** K1, inc 1, knit to last stitch, inc 1, k1. Repeat last 2 rows once more. Knit 1 row. Bind off.

Bottom border With MC and RS facing, pick up and knit 201 stitches at bottom edge of afghan. Continue as for Top border, beginning with row 2.

Side borders With MC and RS facing, pick up and knit 1 stitch in every other row along edge. Continue as for Top border, beginning with row 2.

Finishing

Sew borders together at corners.

Diamond Chart

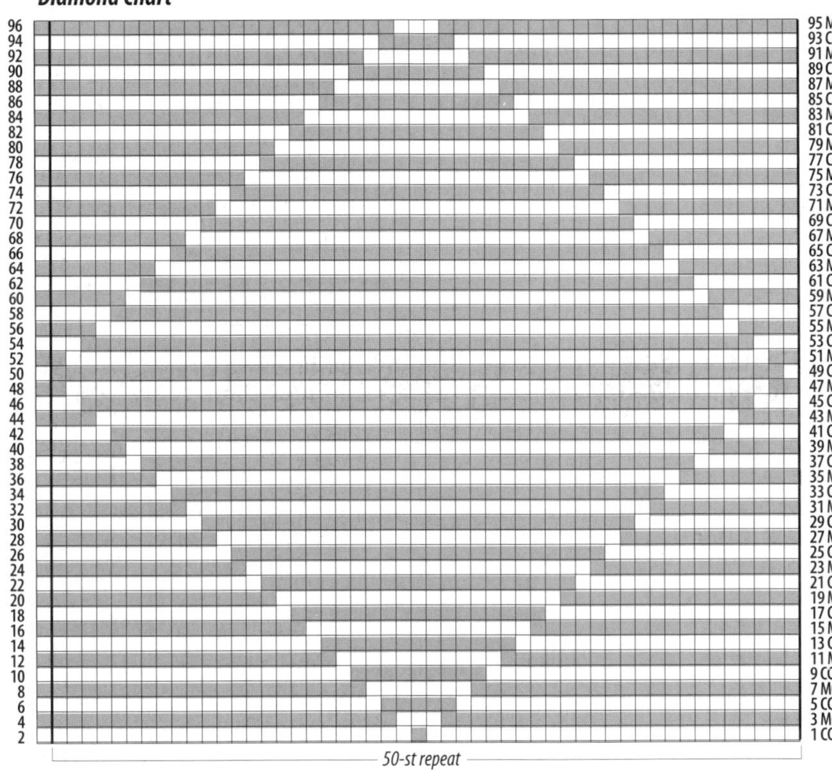

Swatch Chart

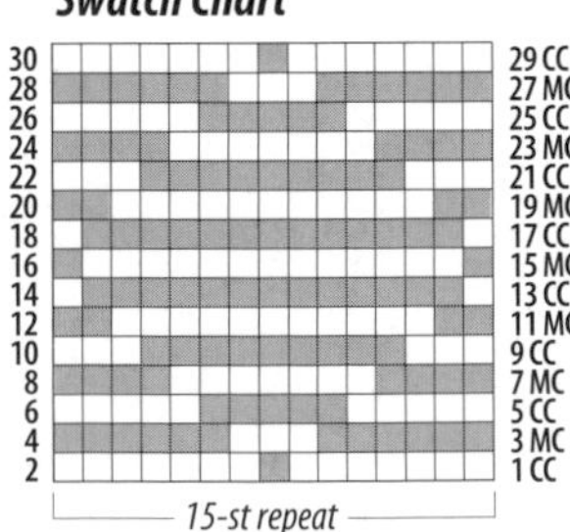

Stitch key

☐ *Knit on RS and WS*
■ *Purl on RS and WS*

Chart notes

1 Change colors at beginning of every RS row.
2 For ease of working, mark RS of work.

Heart Chart

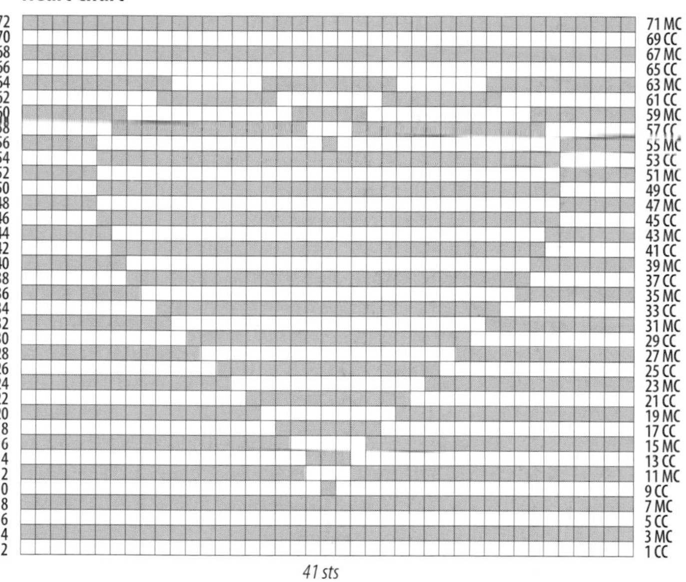

Knitting this 2-color fabric is much easier than it looks. It feels especially lush and cushy, even in a basic, bulky wool. And it's reversible! Try knitting this simple chart; you'll create a red heart on one side and an orange heart on the other.

Elemental Miters

Designed by
Edie Eckman

INTERMEDIATE

Afghan 45" × 56"
Pillows 14" × 14"

10cm/4"

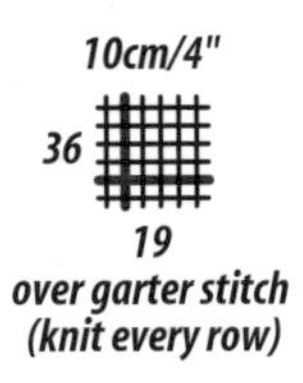

36

19

over garter stitch (knit every row)

1 2 3 **4** 5 6

Medium weight
Afghan
A • 985 yds
B • 788 yds
C • 1182 yds
Pillows
A & C • 394 yds each
B • 197 yds

5mm/US 8, or size to obtain gauge

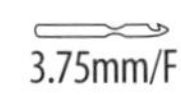

3.75mm/F

&
• tapestry needle
• 14" square pillow form

LION BRAND Wool Ease (80% acrylic, 20% wool; 3oz/85g; 197yd/180m) in 152 Oxford Gray (A), 99 Fisherman (B), 181 Berry Heather (C)

NOTES

1 See *School*, page 102, for cable cast-on, k2tog, SK2P, slip-stitch crochet, and overcast seams. **2** Use cable cast-on throughout. **3** Pick up stitches with RS of work facing. **4** Pick up or cast on stitches for all squares, triangles, and for striped rectangles with A; pick up stitches for basic rectangles with C. **5** Numbers after basic shapes in instructions indicate the order in which the shapes are worked. **6** Pillow cover must be really stretched over form.

Basic Square (BS)

With A, pick up or cast on 31 stitches as directed. ***Row 1 and all WS rows*** Knit with color of previous row. ***Row 2*** With B, k14, SK2P, k14—29 stitches. ***Row 4*** With A, k13, SK2P, k13—27 stitches. ***Row 6*** With B, k12, SK2P, k12—25 stitches. Continue in this way, alternating color every RS row, and working 1 fewer knit stitches before and after center decrease, until there are 3 stitches, end with a WS row. ***Row 30*** (RS) With A, SK2P. Fasten off.

Basic Triangle (BT)

With A, pick up or cast on 31 stitches, as directed ***Row 1 and all WS rows*** Knit with color of previous row. ***Row 2*** With B, k2tog, k12, SK2P, k12, k2tog—27 stitches. ***Row 4*** With A, k2tog, k10, SK2P, k10, k2tog—23 stitches. ***Row 6*** With B, k2tog, k8, SK2P, k8, k2tog—19 stitches. ***Row 8*** With A, k2tog, k6, SK2P, k6, k2tog—15 stitches. ***Row 10*** With B, k2tog, k4, SK2P, k4, k2tog—11 stitches. ***Row 12*** With A, k2tog, k2, SK2P, k2, k2tog—7 stitches. ***Row 14*** With B, k2tog, SK2P, k2tog—3 stitches. ***Row 16*** With B, SK2P. Fasten off.

Basic Rectangle (BR)

With C, pick up and knit (pu&k) 31 stitches, as directed. Knit 29 rows. Bind off.

Striped Rectangle (SR)

With A, pick up or cast on 62 stitches, as directed. ***Row 1 and all WS rows*** Knit with color of previous row. ***Row 2*** With B, k14, SK2P, k28, SK2P, k14—58 stitches. ***Row 4*** With A, k13, SK2P, k26, SK2P, k13—54 stitches. ***Row 6*** With B, k12, SK2P, k24, SK2P, k12—50 stitches. Continue in this way, alternating color every RS row, and working 1 fewer knit stitches before first decrease and after last decrease, and 2 fewer stitches between decreases, until there are 6 stitches, end with a WS row. ***Row 30*** (RS) With A, [SK2P] twice. ***Row 31*** With A, k2tog. Fasten off.

Center Square (CS)

With A, cast on 61 stitches. ***Row 1 and all WS rows*** Knit with color of previous row. ***Row 2*** With B, k29, SK2P, k29—59 stitches. ***Row 4*** With A, k28, SK2P, k28—57 stitches. ***Row 6*** With B, k27, SK2P, k27—55 stitches. Continue in this way, alternating color every RS row, and working 1 fewer knit stitches before and after center decrease, until there are 3 stitches, end with a WS row. ***Row 60*** (RS) With B, SK2P. Fasten off.

PILLOWS

(**Pillow Note** Pillows can be made using the same pattern for the front and back, or mix it up making each side a different pattern.)

Pillow A *(Center Unit)*
SR1 Cast on 62. Work SR.
SR2 Cast on 16, then pu&k 30 along lower (center) edge of SR1, cast on 16—62 stitches. Work SR.

Pillow B *(Center Unit)*
CS1 Cast on 61. Work CS.

Pillow C *(Center Unit)*
BS1 Cast on 31. Work BS.
BS2 Hold BS1 with row 30 at upper right corner. Pu&k 16 along upper edge, then cast on 15. Work BS.
BS3 Cast on 15, then pu&k 16 along right side of BS1. Work BS.
BS4 Pu&k 15 along upper edge of BS3, 1 in corner, and 15 along side of BS2. Work BS.

Pillow D *(Center Unit)*
SR1 and ***SR2*** (worked separately) Cast on 62. Work SR. Sew rectangles together so that cast-on edge forms the outside of square.

Finishing

Edging
With RS facing, crochet hook and C, work slip stitch around outside edge of each pillow. With WS of 2 patterns together, overcast edges together with C, inserting pillow form before sewing final edge.

Pillow joining diagram

1. Work center unit.

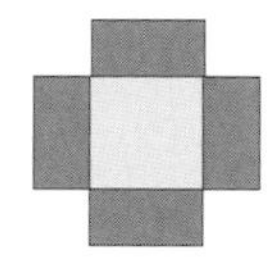

2. Work 4 BR along edges of center unit, following diagram.

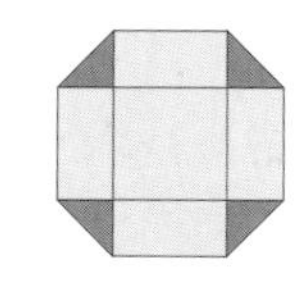

3. Work 4 BT between rectangles, pu&k 15 along side edge of one rectangle, 1 in corner, and 15 along side edge of the next rectangles.

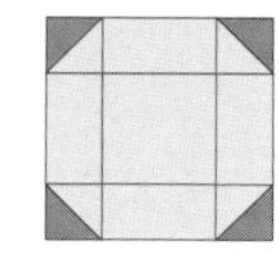

4. Work 4 BT, casting on 31 stitches for each, and sew onto corners of pillow.

Top to bottom: Pillow B, C, and D. Pillow A shown with afghan on page 91.

Pillow A

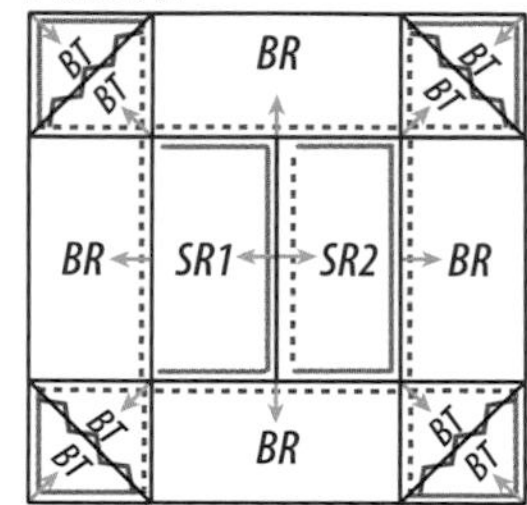

Pillow B

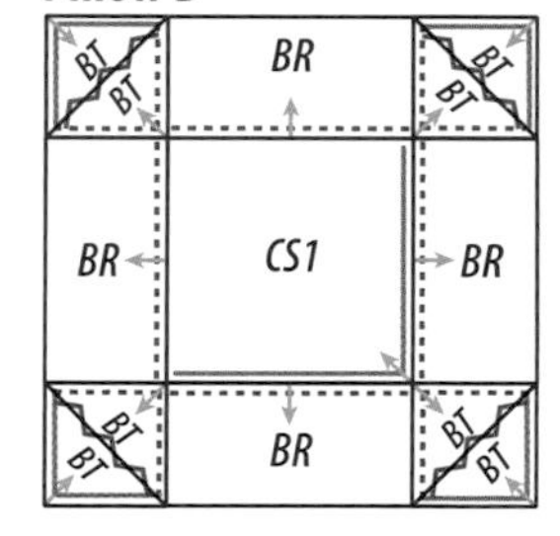

Pillow C

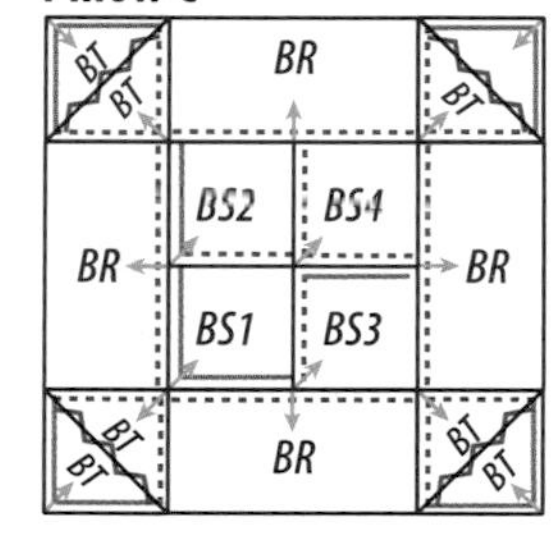

Pillow D

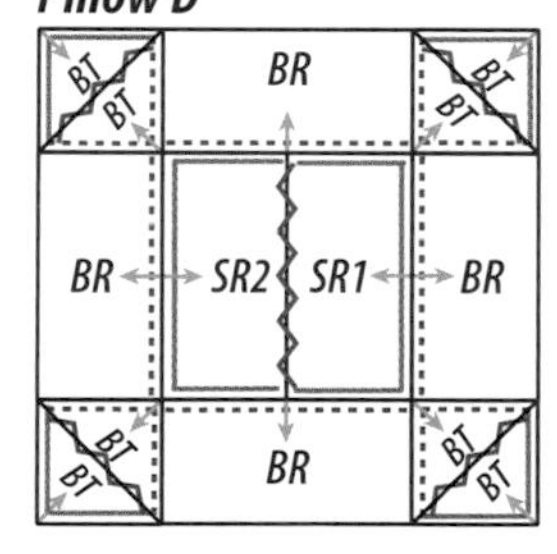

→ *Direction of work*
— *Cast on*
---- *Pick up stitch*
ᴧᴧᴧ *Seam*

AFGHAN

Unit A *(Make 3)*

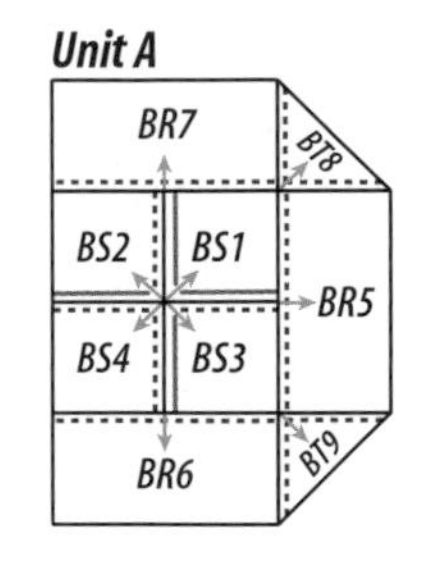

BS1 Cast on 31. Work BS.

BS2 Hold BS1 with row 30 at upper right corner. Pu&k 16 along left edge of BS1, cast on 15. Work BS.

BS3 Cast on 15, then pu&k 1 in corner between BS1 and BS2, and then 15 along lower edge of BS1. Work BS.

BS4 Pu&k 15 along lower edge of BS2, 1 in corner, and 15 along edge of BS3. Work BS.

BR5 Work BR along edges of BS1 and BS3.

BR6 Work BR along edges of BS3 and BS4.

BR7 Work BR along edges of BS1 and BS2.

BT8 Pu&k 15 along side edge of BR5, 1 in corner, and 15 along side edge of BR7. Work BT.

BT9 Pu&k 15 along side edge of BR6, 1 in corner, and 15 along side edge of BR5. Work BT.

Unit B *(Make 2)*

Work BS1, BS2, BS3, BS4 and BR5 as for Unit A.

BR6 Work BR along edges of BS2 and BS4.

BT7 Pu&k 16 along side edge of BR6, cast on 15. Work BT.

BT8 Cast on 15, then pu&k 16 along side edge of BR5. Work BT.

BT9 Cast on 15, then pu&k 16 along side edge of BR6. Work BT.

BT10 Pu&k 16 along side edge of BR5, cast on 15. Work BT.

Unit C *(Make 3)*

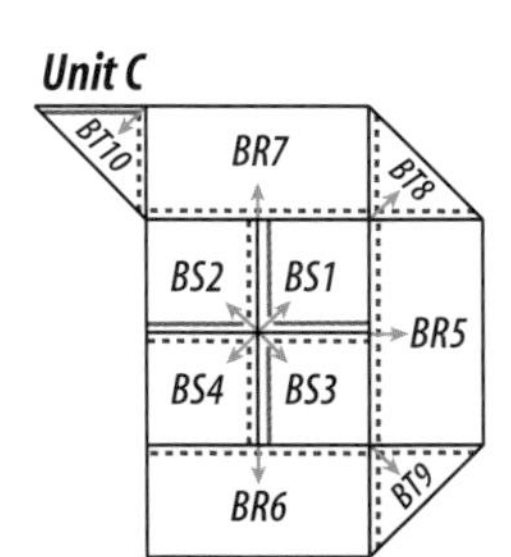

Work Unit A.

BT10 Cast on 15, then pu&k 16 along side edge of BR7. Work BT.

Unit D *(Make 6)*

Work BS1, BS2, BS3, BS4 and BR5 as for Unit A.

BT6 Work as for BT8 of Unit B.

BT7 Work as for BT10 of Unit B.

Unit E *(Make 3)*

Work Unit A.

BR10 Work BR along edges of BS2 and BS4.

BT11 Pu&k 15 along side edge of BR10, 1 in corner, then 15 along side edge of BR6. Work BT.

BT12 Pu&k 15 along side edge of BR7, 1 in corner, then 15 along side edge of BR10. Work BT.

Unit F *(Make 3)*

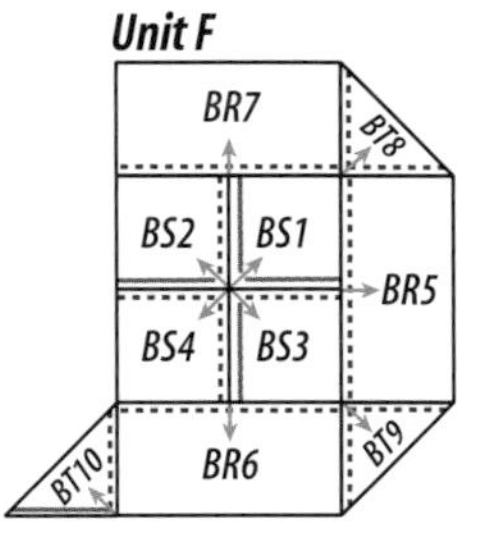

Work Unit A.

BT10 Pu&k 16 along side edge of BR6, then cast on 15. Work BT.

Unit G (Make 4)

Cast on 31. Work BT.

Finishing

Sew units together, following Joining Diagram.

Edging

With RS facing, crochet hook and C, work slip stitch into each edge stitch around. Fasten off.

→ *Direction of work*
— *Cast on*
---- *Pick up stitch*

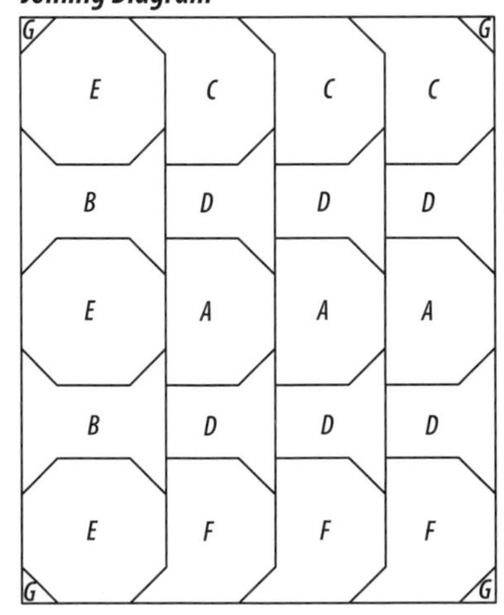

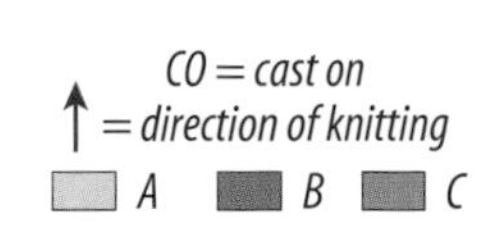

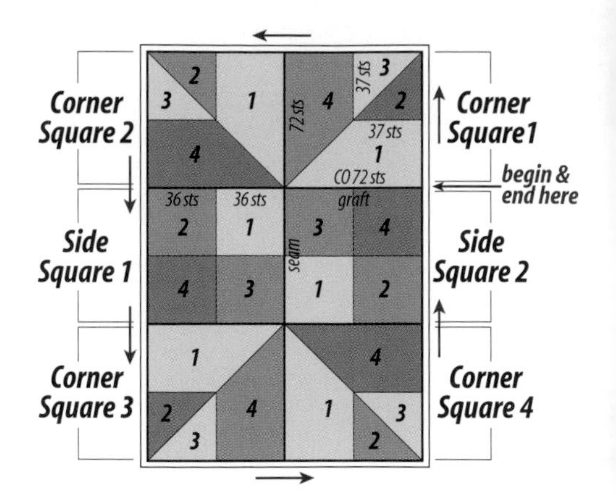

Outer Limit

Designed by
Colleen Smitherman

INTERMEDIATE +

42" wide × 60" long

10cm/4"

23

14

over stockinette stitch (knit on RS, purl on WS)

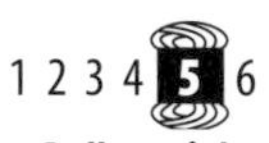

Bulky weight
A • 525 yds
B • 320 yds
C • 425 yds

5.5mm/US 9, or size to obtain gauge

COATS & CLARK TLC Amore (80% acrylic, 20% nylon; 6oz/127g; 290yd/265m) in 3625 Celery (A), 3628 Dark Thyme (B), 3534 Plum (C)

Notes

1 See *School*, page 102, for invisible cast-on, knit in row below (k1b), short rows, grafting, and intarsia. **2** At beginning of RS rows, slip stitches purlwise with yarn in back. **3** Afghan consists of 4 Corner Squares and 2 Side Squares; each square has 4 color sections. Follow diagram for colors to use in each section. **4** Corner Squares are shaped with short rows. **5** When working Side Squares, bring new color under old at color change.

Hide Wrap (HW) Knit next stitch and its wrap together.
Hide 2 Wraps (H2W) Knit next stitch and its 2 wraps together.

CORNER SQUARE

First section

Begin short-row shaping: Rows 1, 3, 5, 7, 9, 11 and 13 (WS) Purl to last 9 stitches, [k1b, p1] 4 times, p1. ***Row 2*** Sl 1, knit to last 2 stitches, wrap next stitch & turn (W&T). ***Rows 4, 6, 8, 10 and 12*** Sl 1, knit to 1 stitch before last wrapped stitch, W&T. ***Row 4*** Sl 1, knit to 2 stitches before last wrapped stitch, W&T. ***Rows 15, 17, 19, 21, 23 and 25*** Repeat row 3. ***Rows 16, 18, 20, 22 and 24*** Repeat row 4. Repeat rows 14–25 three times more—37 stitches worked on last row.

Second section

Change color. Work rows 14–25 of first section five times (last 12 rows will begin to cut into 9-stitch border pattern). ***Next row*** (RS) Slip 1, W&T. ***Next row*** Purl 1.

Third section

(**Note** Do not hide wraps in purl ribs of 9-stitch border.)
Change color. ***Row 1*** (RS) Sl 1, HW, W&T. ***Row 2*** Purl 2. ***Row 3*** Sl 1, k2, W&T. ***Row 4*** K1b, p2. ***Row 5*** Sl 1, k2, H2W, W&T. ***Row 6*** P1, k1b, p2. ***Row 7*** Sl 1, k4, W&T. ***Row 8*** [K1b, p1] twice, p1. ***Row 9*** Sl 1, k4, H2W, k1, W&T. ***Row 10*** [K1b, p1] 3 times, p1. ***Row 11*** Sl 1, k6, H2W, W&T. ***Row 12*** [P1, k1b] 3 times, p2. ***Row 13*** Sl 1, k8, W&T. ***Row 14*** [K1b, p1] 4 times, p1. ***Rows 15, 17 and 19*** Sl 1, knit to next double-wrapped knit stitch, H2W, W&T. ***Rows 16, 18, 20, 22 and 24*** Purl to last 9 stitches, [k1b, p1] 4 times, p1. ***Row 21*** Sl 1, knit to next double-wrapped knit stitch, H2W, HW, W&T. ***Row 23*** Repeat row 15. ***Row 25*** Sl 1, knit to next single-wrapped knit stitch, HW, W&T. ***Row 26*** Repeat row 16. Repeat rows 15–26 three times more—37 stitches worked on last row.

Fourth section

Change color. Work rows 15–26 of third section four times, then repeat rows 15–24 once more. ***Next row*** (RS) Sl 1, knit to last stitch, HW.

SIDE SQUARE

First and second sections

Row 1 (WS) With color of first section, p36, then with color of second section, purl to last 9 stitches, [k1b, p1] 4 times, p1. ***Row 2*** Sl 1, knit to end, matching colors. Repeat these 2 rows 26 times more.

Third and fourth sections

Row 1 (WS) With color of third section, p36, then with color of fourth section, purl to last 9 stitches, [k1b, p1] 4 times, p1. ***Row 2*** Sl 1, knit to end, matching colors. Repeat these 2 rows 26 times more.

AFGHAN

With A and using invisible cast-on, cast on 72 stitches. Purl 1 row on WS. Work Corner Square 1 (beginning with row 2), Corner Square 2, Side Square 1, Corner Square 3, Corner Square 4, and Side Square 2.

Finishing

Place cast-on stitches onto needle, removing waste yarn. Being careful not to twist afghan, graft beginning and end stitches together with A. Seam Side Squares 1 and 2 together at center. Lightly steam, expanding ribbed edge slightly and shaping corners.

Try your own colors online at
www.KnittingUniverse.com/PAINTBOX.

Knitter's Handbook

Easy as Pi Pillows

Designed by **Susan Douglas**

INTERMEDIATE

Small pillow • 12" diameter
Large pillow • 14" diameter

10cm/4"

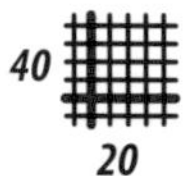

20
over garter stitch (knit every row)

Medium weight
A–D • 230 yds each
(makes both pillows)

4mm/US 6, or size to obtain gauge

four 4mm/US 6

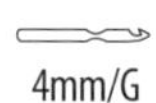

4mm/G

four 1½" (38mm) shank buttons

fiberfill for stuffing

PLYMOUTH YARN CO Galway (100% wool; 3½ oz/100g; 230 yd/207m) in 109 Beige (A), 105 Denim (B), 10 Seafoam (C), 94 Brown (D)

Notes

1 See *School*, page 102, for chain cast-on, wrap & turn (W&T), working with double-pointed needles (dpn), and garter-stitch grafting. **2** Instructions are for smaller pillow with changes for larger pillow in parentheses.

Pillow

Section 1

With A, chain cast on 62 (70) stitches; cast-on counts as row 1. ***Begin short rows: Row 2*** (WS) K61 (69), W&T. ***Row 3*** K60 (68), W&T. ***Row 4*** K58 (66), W&T. ***Row 5*** K56 (64), W&T. Continue in this way, working 2 fewer stitches every row through row 21 (25). ***Row 22 (26)*** (WS) K25, W&T. ***Row 23 (27)*** K26, W&T. ***Row 24 (28)*** K28, W&T. ***Row 25 (29)*** K30, W&T. Continue working 2 more stitches each row through row 41 (49). ***Row 42 (50)*** (WS) K62 (70). Cut A, join B.

Sections 2–8

* Knit 1 row, then work rows 2–42 (2–50) once. Repeat from * 5 times more, using C, D, A, B and C (7 sections total). With D, knit 1 row, then work rows 2–41 (2–49). Cut yarn, leaving approximately 1½ yards for grafting.

Finishing

Remove waste chain and with D, garter-stitch graft open stitches of first and last sections together, stuffing pillow before it is closed completely. Run a length of yarn through center stitches and pull together to close center.

Button cover (Make 2)

With desired color, cast on 22 stitches and divide evenly over 3 dpns. Join, being careful not to twist stitches. Knit 7 rounds. ***Next round*** K2tog around. Break yarn, pull through remaining stitches and secure. Place cover over button, run a length of yarn through cast-on stitches and gather around shank. Sew button to center of one side of pillow, then run yarn through pillow to other side and sew 2nd button to center of other side of pillow.

Try your own colors online at
www.KnittingUniverse.com/PAINTBOX.

Choices

A well-appointed home complements your lifestyle and reflects your personality. Its contents are a result of your evolving sense of color and style. Whether you proceed cautiously on familiar ground or take off fearlessly in a new direction, you face choices.

You can make those choices; you don't need to consult an expert. Catalogs, books, and magazines are full of inspiration. Something catches your eye — a color, a motif, whatever. Translate it into a knit for your home.

color

The bed and bath section of a department store is a great place to scout color trends. Or gather a few chips at a paint store. Of course, the yarn shop with its rainbow of yarn is your destination.

Choose colors that speak to you. Introduce new colors in small amounts. Take a hue from a piece of artwork, then pick a yarn that matches. Let that yarn live in the room for a while. If you love it, translate it into a pillow, a border, or your next afghan. If not, replace it; you will be surprised how easily you can create an exciting new mix.

gauge

Gauge is important in sizing a garment, but it is not as crucial for home décor. Use the swatch as an exploration point; just make sure to create a fabric suitable for the project. A single pattern can be worked at different gauges, each in a different yarn, for a series pillows in graduated sizes — all with the same number of stitches and rows.

The Adobe Bricks afghan shines in browns and purples; work intarsia with one variegated yarn in the Americana cushion; and finish your look with the Pita Pillow in purple.

yarns

The yarns we used may not be available to you or to your liking, but that's not a problem. Find something similar or something you prefer. Use yarns you love. Although you might not care to work a particular yarn into a sweater, it could be fun in a home accessory.

coordinates

Decorator and quilt fabrics can set the mood of a room. Why not use them for pillow backs, coordinating pillows, or as a starting point? A half-yard of fabric can easily be assembled into a cushion. Or try a piece of suede or leather.

one piece or many

Any stitch pattern can be expanded or isolated. For minimal finishing, choose one piece. For easy portability and almost-instant gratification, work a large piece in sections. Work additional pieces for an even larger project or fewer for a smaller one. If you don't relish the thought of sewing many blocks together, join them as you go. Knit 4, block, and sew them together; they will look good and keep you motivated. They might even look like a pillow...

A quick look at our pillow and afghan sets will convince you how easy it is. Turn a pillow pattern into an afghan repeat or vice versa. Often the pleasure in making the pillow will help you commit to the afghan.

Finishing

For knit garments, we often worry about the right buttons, neat seams, the perfect border and bind-off. Even more important is the whole issue of making a sweater fit.

Finishing a knit for your home is less stressful. If gauge isn't precise and the finished afghan is a few inches shorter or wider, it's usually not noticed, very rarely an issue. A knitted pillow looks best when it fits snugly over the stuffing. And if it is too big, just make a bigger pillow.

swatching

Before you begin your afghan or pillow you should make a swatch to see how the pattern works as well as to determine gauge. Once the swatch is made, make sure to wash and block it. If it needs to be pinned to shape, do so. You want this to be a preview of your larger project. Every step of preparation assures success later.

blocking

Washing a large afghan is not a daunting task. Modern times have provided us with no-rinse formulas and washing machines. Fill the washer

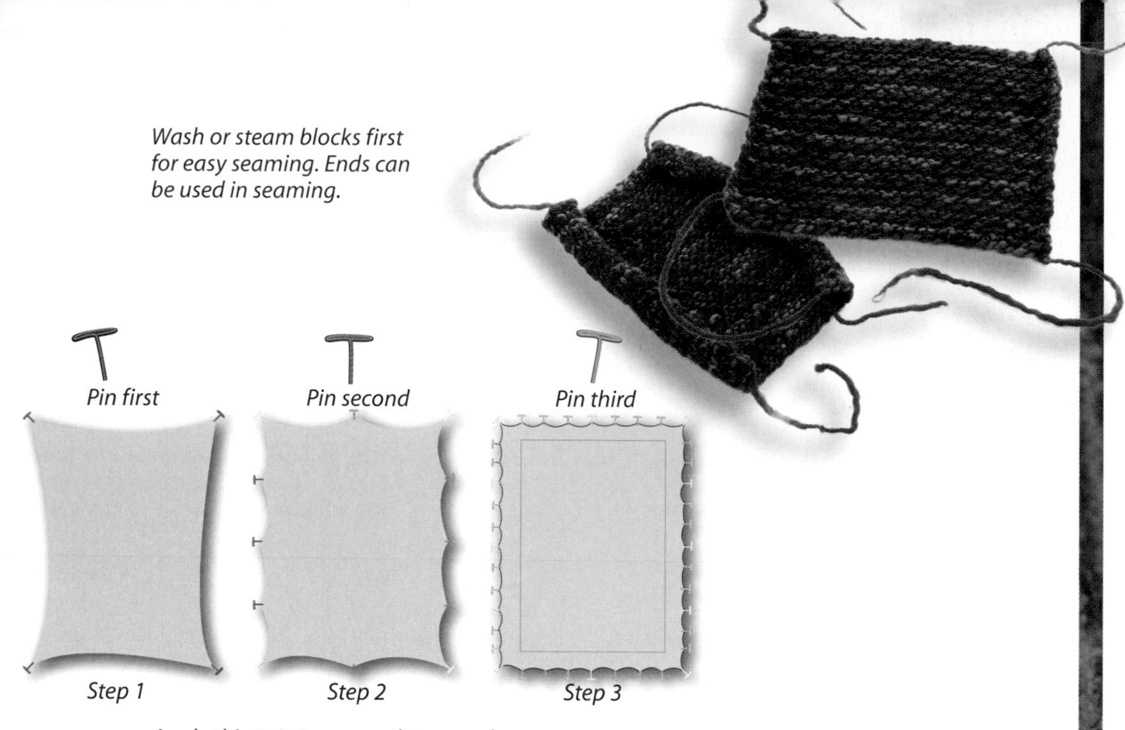

Wash or steam blocks first for easy seaming. Ends can be used in seaming.

Apply this 1–2–3 approach to any shape.

with tepid water and add your wool wash; turn the machine off. Place the knit into the machine and let it soak; 20 minutes should be sufficient. Next, set the washer to drain (make sure that it does not agitate or add water) and then spin out excess water. Remove your knit and lay out flat to dry. Pin it out if necessary (see illustration).

Laying out the piece may be an issue if you are short of space. A floor works well, or even the top of a bed as long as you make sure to protect it from the moisture. Use a plastic drop cloth or shower curtain under a sheet or towels.

seaming

Afghans and pillows should be pieced together neatly and securely. They require a flexible seam that will wear well. You can seam in different ways. Just make sure to neaten all ends and weave them into the seams as well. The true sign of great finishing is seams that do not constrict the drape of the fabric; although visible, they are neat and tidy.

Take time to finish your knits with all the care and love you give your knitting. They will last a lifetime and become true heirlooms for your loved ones.

MATTRESS STITCH

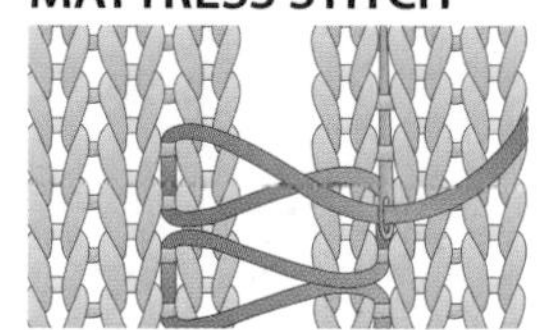

GARTER RIDGE JOIN

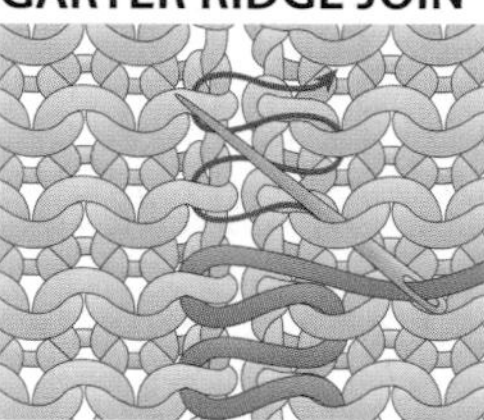

CAST-ON TO BIND-OFF

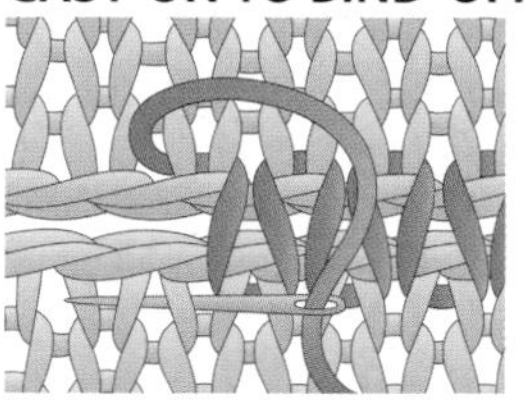

STOCKINETTE SIDE TO BIND-OFF

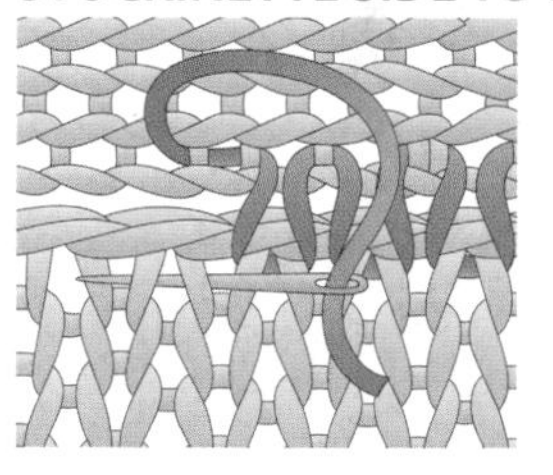

GARTER SIDE TO BIND-OFF

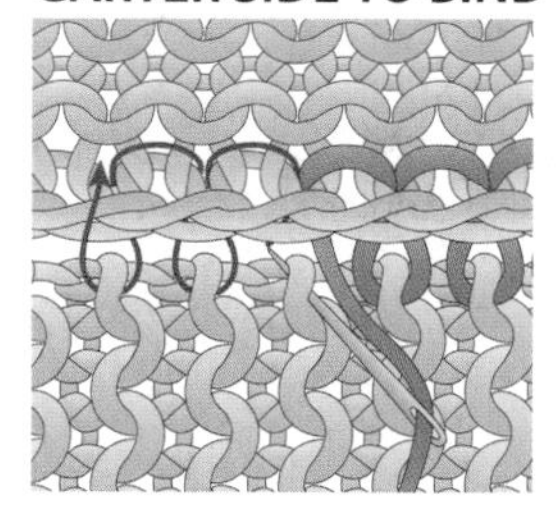

OVERCAST SEAM

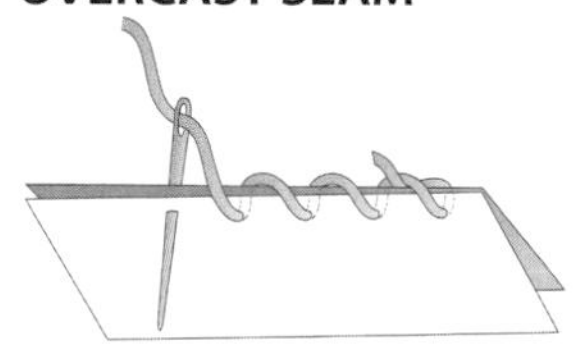

SLIP-ST CROCHET SEAM

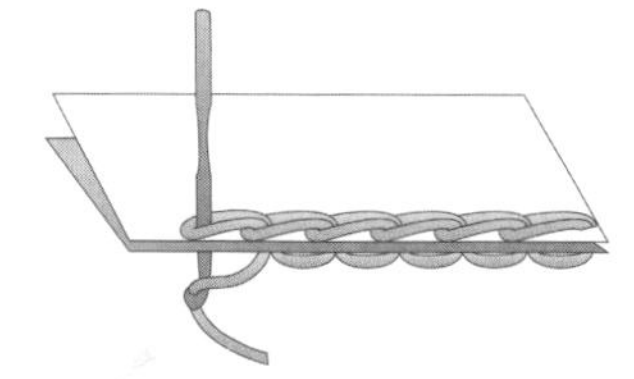

School Index

Cast-ons

CIRCLE CAST-ON

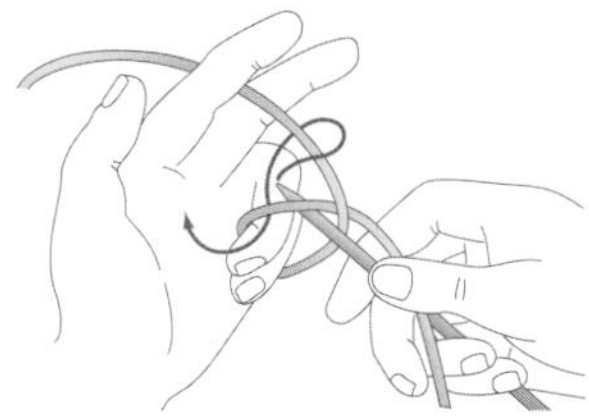

1 Holding tail in right hand and yarn in left hand, make a circle with tail **behind** yarn in left hand.
2 Insert double-pointed needle in circle and draw yarn through,

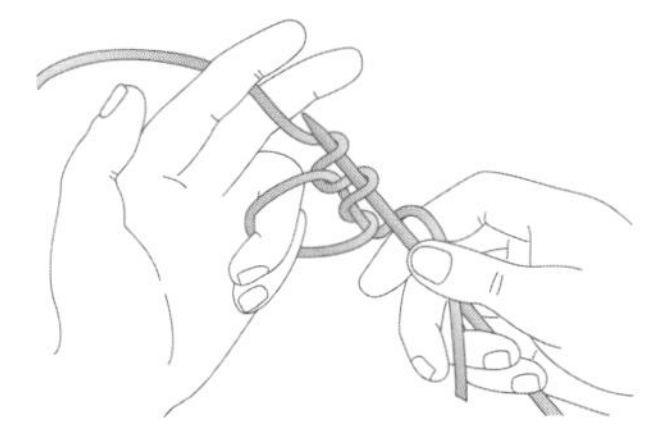

forming a stitch on needle. Do not remove fingers from loop.
3 Bring yarn from front to back over needle, forming a yarn-over on needle.

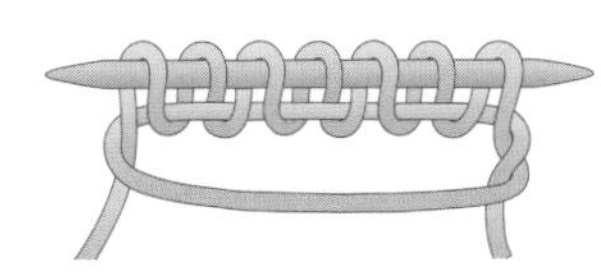

4 Repeat Steps 2 and 3, ending with Step 2 (and an odd number of stitches).
5 Arrange stitches on double-pointed needles, pulling tail slightly to tighten.

LONG-TAIL CAST-ON

Make a slip knot for the initial stitch, at a distance from the end of the yarn, allowing about 1½" for each stitch to be cast on.
1 Bring yarn between fingers of left hand and wrap around little finger as shown.

2 Bring left thumb and index finger between strands, arranging so tail is on thumb side, ball strand on finger side. Open thumb and finger so strands form a diamond.

3 Bring needle down, forming a loop around thumb.
4 Bring needle **under** front strand of **thumb loop**...

5...up **over index finger yarn**, catching it...

6...and bringing it **under** the front of **thumb loop**.

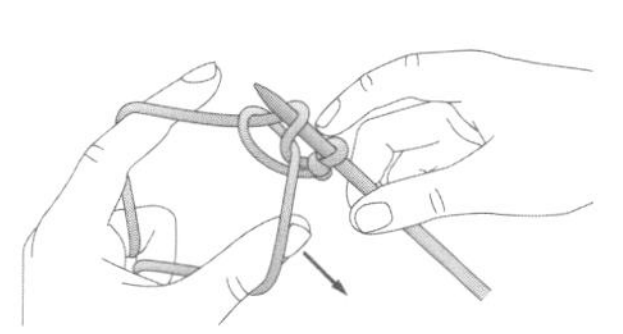

7 Slip thumb out of its loop, and use thumb to adjust tension on the new stitch. One knit stitch cast on.

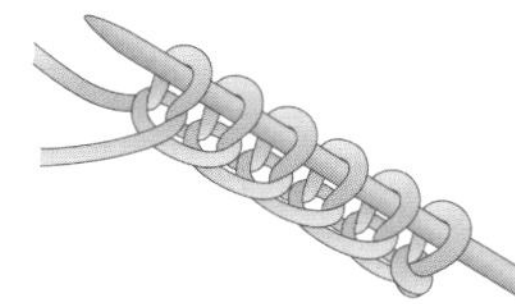

Repeat Steps 3–7 for each additional stitch.

INVISIBLE CAST-ON

A temporary cast-on
1 Knot working yarn to contrasting waste yarn. Hold needle and knot in right hand. Tension both strands in left hand; separate strands so waste yarn is over index finger, working yarn over thumb. Bring needle between strands and under thumb yarn so working yarn forms a yarn-over in front of waste yarn.

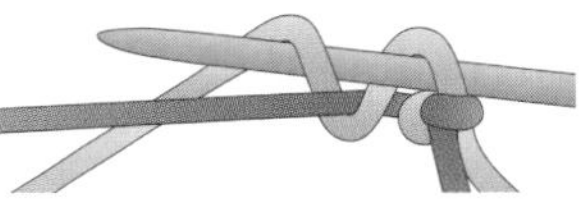
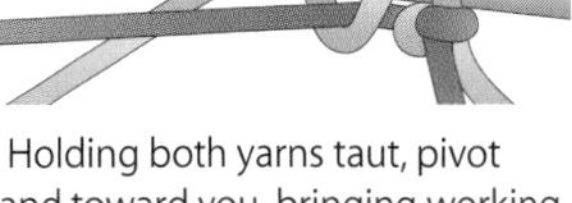
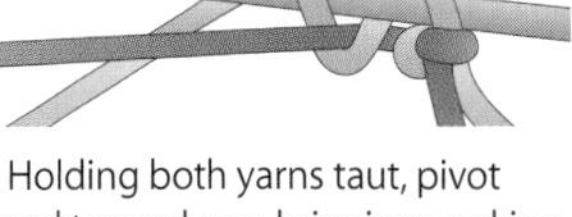

2 Holding both yarns taut, pivot hand toward you, bringing working yarn under and behind waste yarn. Bring needle behind and under working yarn so working yarn forms a yarn-over behind waste yarn.

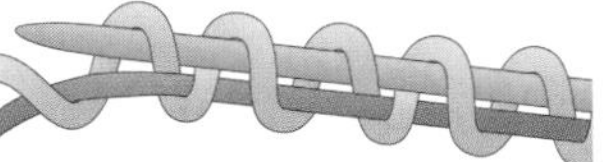

3 Pivot hand away from you, bringing working yarn under and in front of waste yarn. Bring needle between strands and under working yarn, forming a yarn-over in front of waste yarn. Each yarn-over forms a stitch.
Repeat Steps 2–3 for required number of stitches. For an even number, twist working yarn around waste strand before knitting the first row.

CABLE CAST-ON

1–2 Work as for Steps 1 and 2 of Knit Cast-on (page 108).

3 Insert left needle in loop and slip loop off right needle. One additional stitch cast on.

4 Insert right needle **between** the last 2 stitches. From this position, knit a stitch and slip it to the left needle as in Step 3.
Repeat Step 4 for each additional stitch.

LOOP CAST-ON (ALSO CALLED E-WRAP CAST-ON)

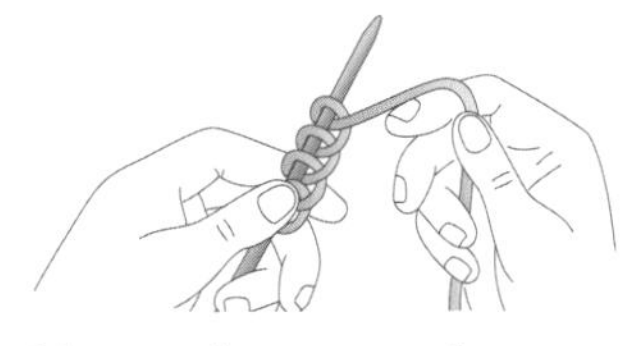

Often used to cast on a few stitches, as for a buttonhole
1 Hold needle and tail in left hand.
2 Bring right index finger under yarn, pointing toward you.

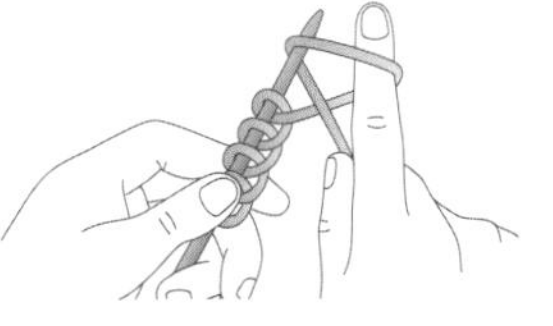

3 Turn index finger to point away from you.
4 Insert tip of needle under yarn on index finger (see above); remove finger and draw yarn snug, forming a stitch.
Repeat Steps 2–4 until all stitches are on needle.

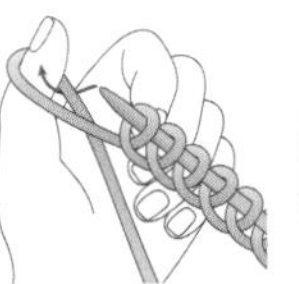

Left-slanting ***Right-slanting***

Loops can be formed over index or thumb and can slant to the left or to the right. On the next row, work through back loop of right-slanting loops

PICKING UP STITCHES IN CHAIN

A temporary cast-on
1 With crochet hook and waste yarn, loosely chain the number of stitches needed, plus a few extra chains. Cut yarn.

2 With needle and main yarn, pick up and knit 1 stitch into the back 'purl bump' of the first chain.

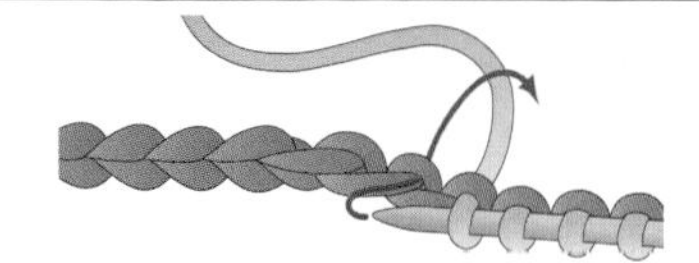

Continue, knitting 1 stitch into each chain until you have the required number of stitches. Do not work into remaining chains.

Increases

KNIT INTO FRONT & BACK OF STITCH (kf&b)

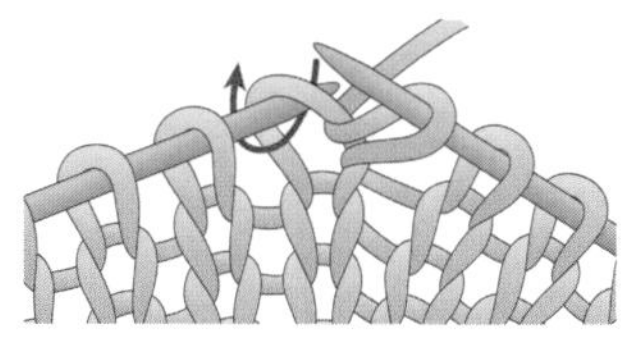

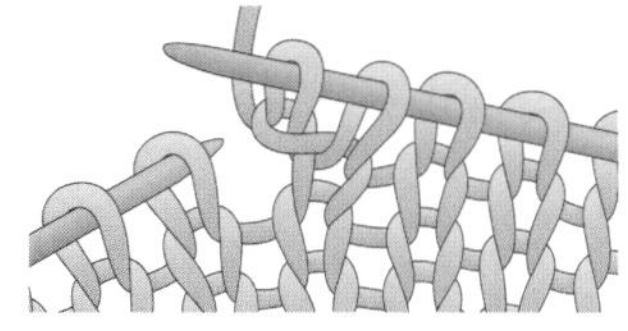

1 Knit into front of next stitch on left needle, but do not pull stitch off needle. ***2*** Take right needle to back, then knit through back of same stitch (as shown above).

3 Now take both stitches off left needle.

LIFTED INCREASE, KNIT OR PURL

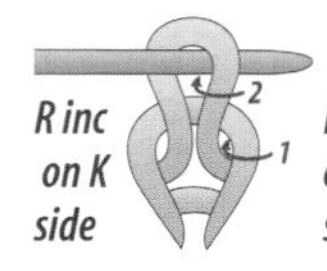

L inc on P side

L inc on K side

R inc on P side

Work increase before stitch
Knit or purl into right loop of stitch in row below next stitch on left needle (1), then knit or purl into stitch on needle (2).

Work increase after stitch
Knit or purl next stitch on left needle, then knit or purl into left loop of stitch in row below this stitch (3).

KOK INCREASE (k1-yo-K1)

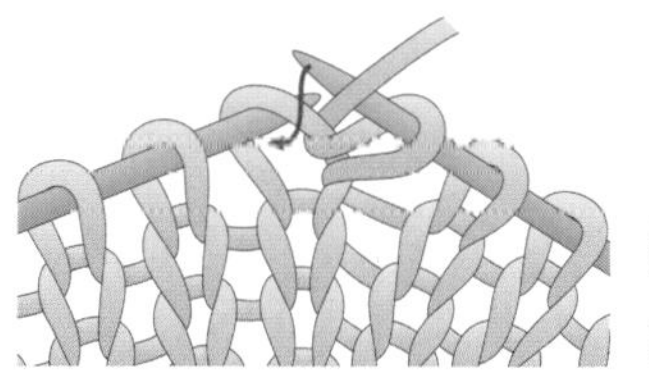

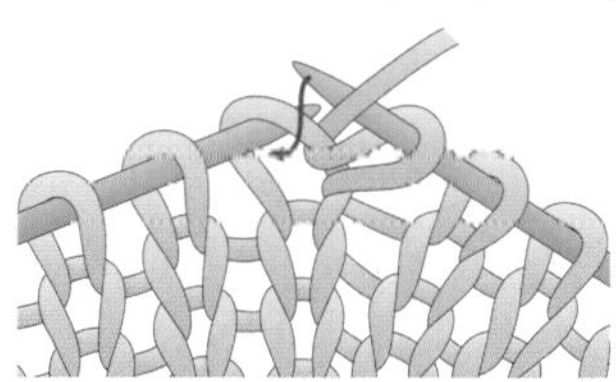

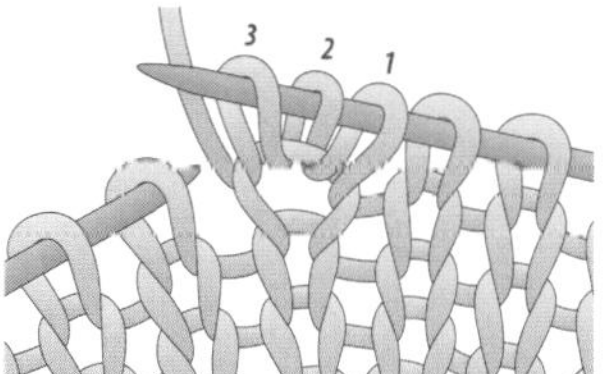

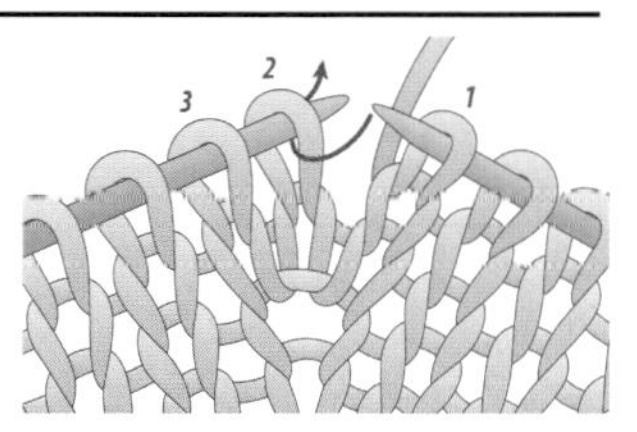

1 Knit 1, leaving stitch on left needle.
2 Bring yarn to front and over needle (creating a yarn over).
3 Knit into the stitch again.

Completed increase: 3 stitches from 1 stitch.

On next increase row, work KOK increase into center stitch of increase of previous increase row.

MAKE 1 LEFT (M1L), KNIT

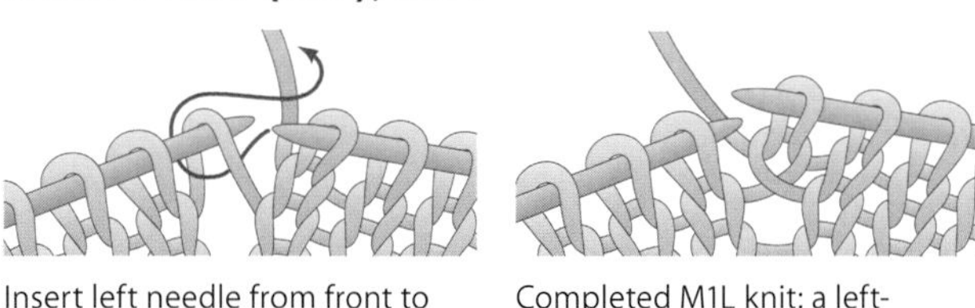

Insert left needle from front to back under strand between last stitch knitted and first stitch on left needle. Knit, twisting strand by working into loop at back of needle.

Completed M1L knit: a left-slanting increase.

YARN OVER (yo)

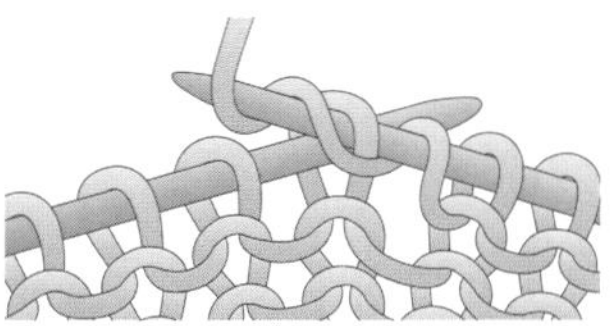

Between knit stitches
Bring yarn under the needle to the front, take it over the needle to the back and knit the next stitch.

Between purl stitches
With yarn in front of needle, bring it over the needle to the back and to the front again; purl next stitch.

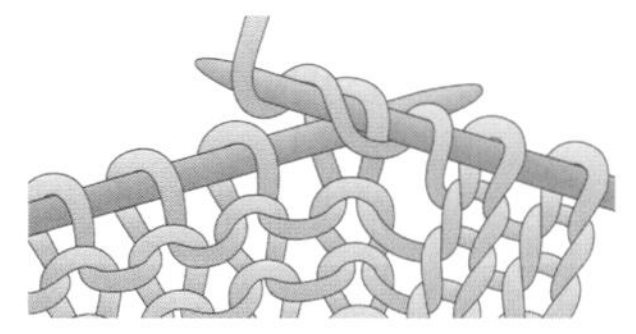

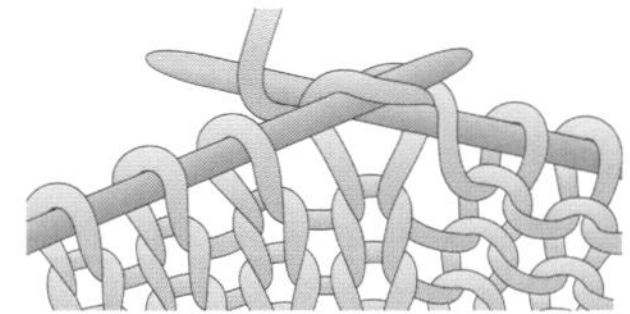

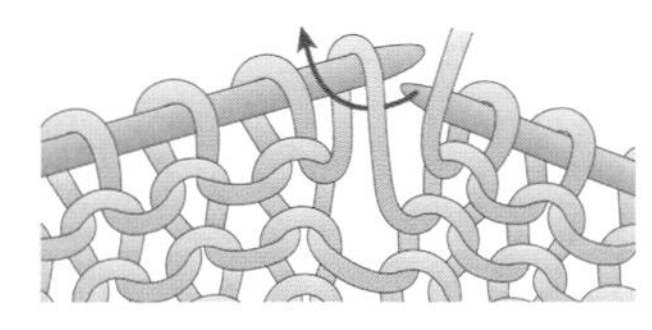

After a knit, before a purl
Bring yarn under the needle to the front, over the needle to the back, then under the needle to the front; purl next stitch.

After a purl, before a knit
With yarn in front of the needle, bring it over the needle to the back; knit next stitch.

On next row
Knit or purl into front of yarn-over unless instructed otherwise. The yarn-over makes a hole and adds a stitch.

MAKE 1 RIGHT (M1R), KNIT

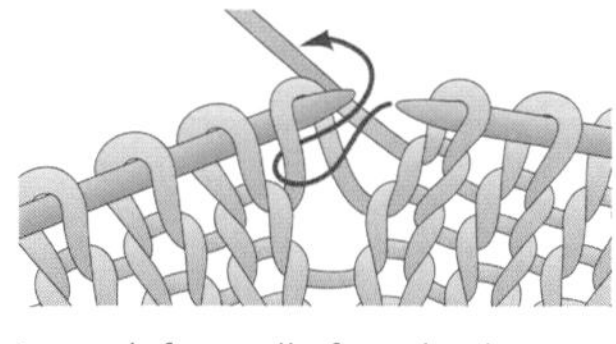

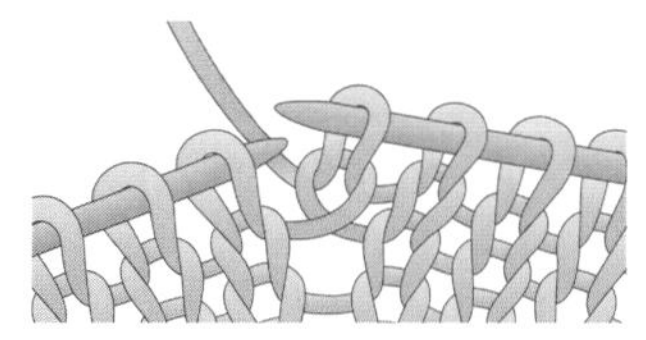

Insert left needle from back to front under strand between last stitch knitted and first stitch on left needle. Knit, twisting the strand by working into loop at front of the needle.

Completed M1R knit: a right-slanting increase.

Abbreviations

BO bind off
CC contrasting color
ch chain
cm centimeter(s)
cn cable needle
CO cast on
dec decreas(e) (ed) (es) (ing)
dpn double-pointed needle(s)
g gram(s)
" inch(es)
inc increas(e) (ed) (es) (ing)
k knit(ting)(s)(ted)
k1b knit one below
k2tog knit 2 together
m meter(s)
M1 Make one stitch (increase)
MC main color
mm millimeter(s)
oz ounce(s)
p purl(ed) (ing) (s)
p1b purl one below
pm place marker
psso pass slipped stitch(es) over
rnd round(s)
sc single crochet
sl slip(ped) (ping)
SKP slip, knit, psso
SSK slip, slip, knit these 2 sts tog
SSP slip, slip, purl these 2 sts tog
st(s) stitch(es)
St st stockinette stitch
tbl through back of loop(s)
tog together
WS wrong side(s)
wyib with yarn in back
wyif with yarn in front
x times
yd(s) yard(s)
yo yarn over (UK yarn forward)

Decreases

S2KP2, sl 2-k1-p2sso

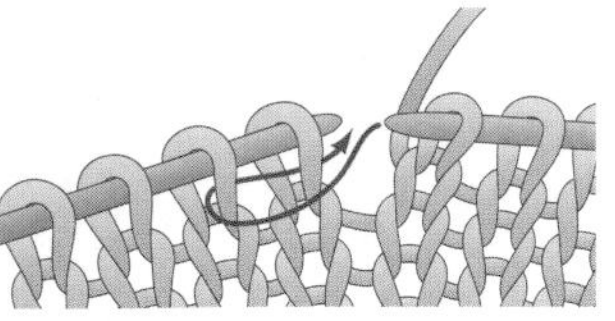

1 Slip 2 stitches ***together*** to right needle as if to knit.

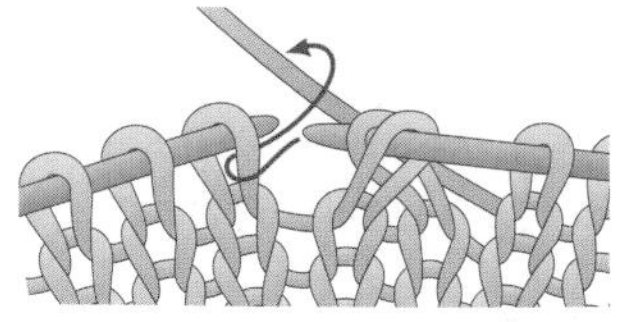

2 Knit next stitch.

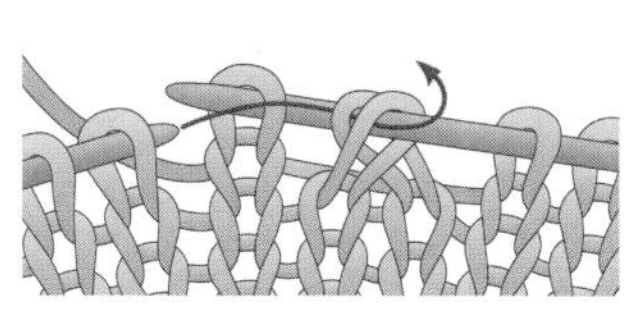

3 Pass 2 slipped stitches over knit stitch and off right needle: 3 stitches become 1; the center stitch is on top.

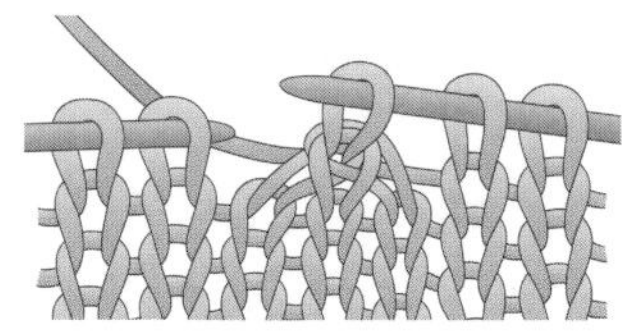

The result is a centered double decrease.

SK2P, sl 1-k2tog-psso

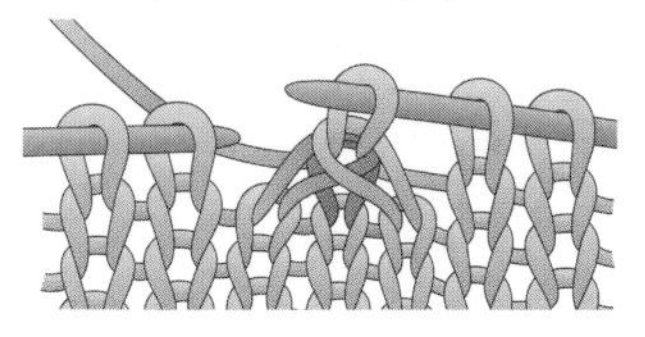

1 Slip 1 stitch knitwise.
2 Knit next 2 stitches together.
3 Pass the slipped stitch over the k2tog: 3 stitches become 1; the right stitch is on top.
The result is a left-slanting double decrease.

SSK

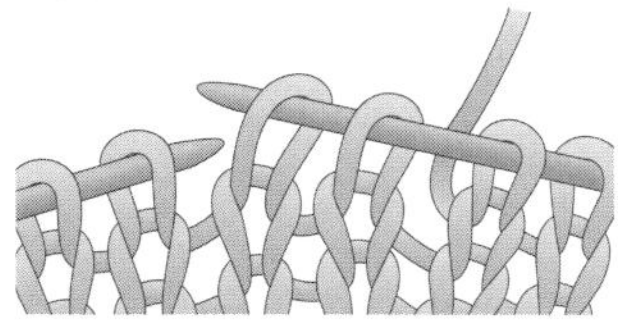

1 Slip 2 stitches ***separately*** to right needle as if to knit.

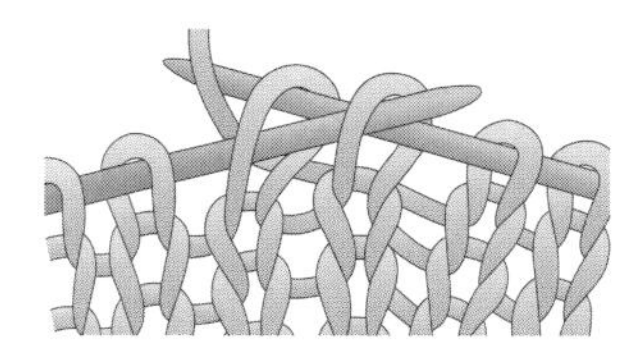

2 Slip left needle into these 2 stitches from left to right and knit them together: 2 stitches become 1.

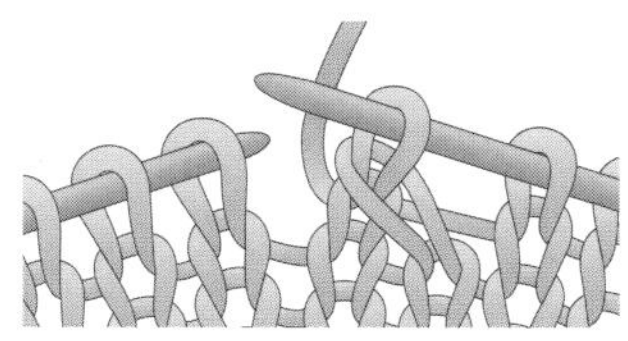

The result is a left-slanting decrease.

SSSK

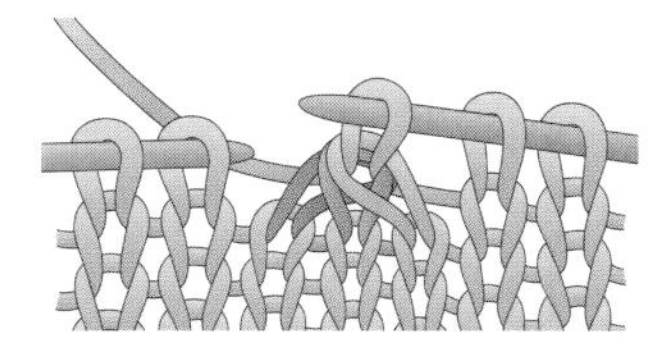

Work same as ***SSK*** EXCEPT:
1 Slip ***3*** stitches....
2 Slip left needle into these ***3*** stitches... ***3*** stitches become 1.
The result is a left-slanting double decrease.

SSP

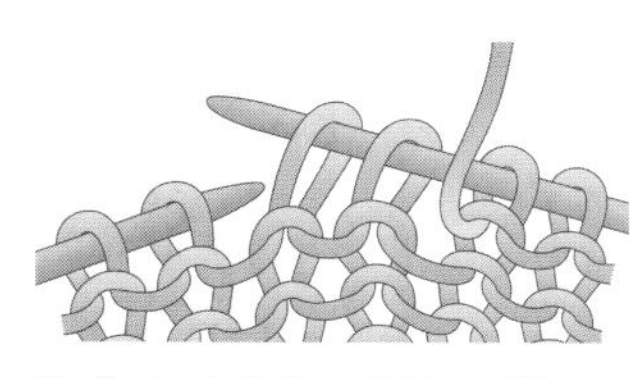

Use instead of p2tog-tbl to avoid twisting the stitches.

1 Slip 2 stitches ***separately*** to right needle as if to knit.

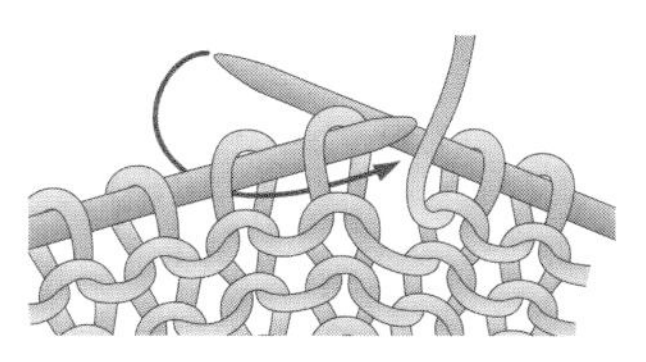

2 Slip these 2 stitches back onto left needle. Insert right needle through their 'back loops,' into the second stitch and then the first.

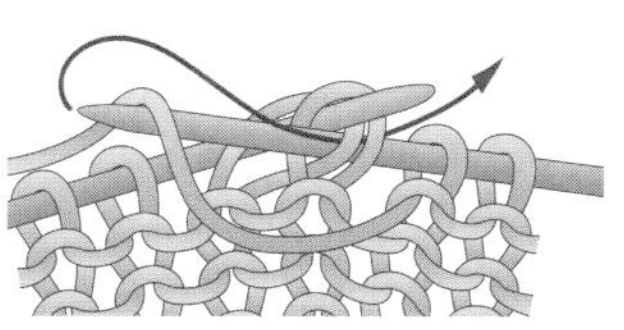

3 Purl them together: 2 stitches become 1.

The result is a left-slanting decrease.

P3TOG

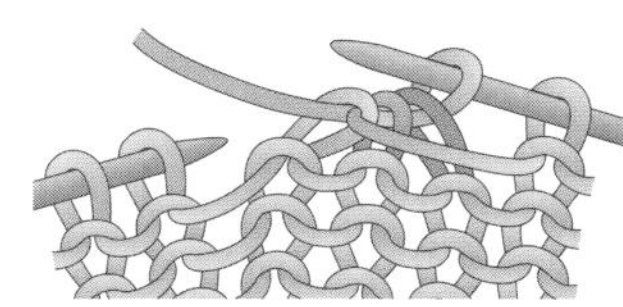

1 Insert right needle into first 3 stitches on left needle.
2 Purl all 3 stitches together, as if they were 1. The result is a right-slanting double decrease.

K2tog

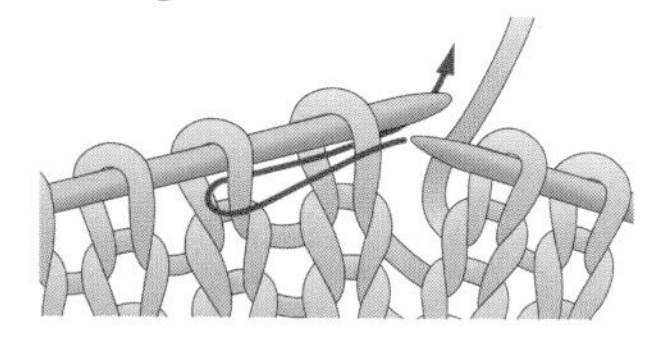

1 Insert right needle into first 2 stitches on left needle, beginning with second stitch from end of left needle.

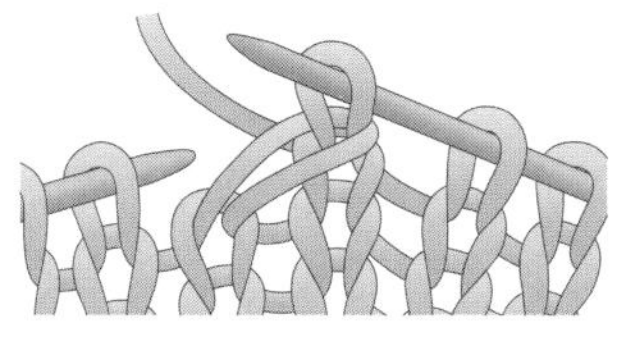

2 Knit these 2 stitches together as if they were 1.
The result is a right-slanting decrease.

P2tog

1 Insert right needle into first 2 stitches on left needle.

2 Purl these 2 stitches together as if they were 1.
The result is a right-slanting decrease.

K3TOG

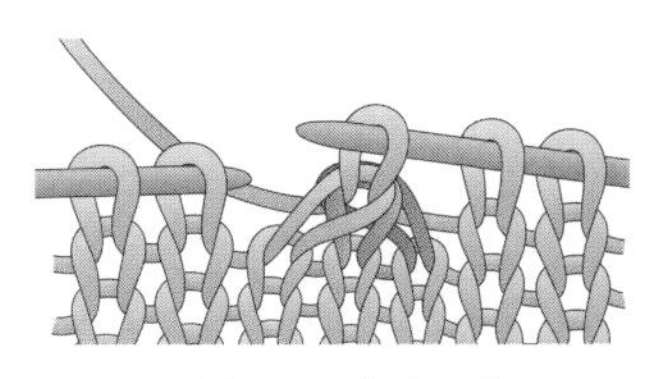

1 Insert right needle into first 3 stitches on left needle, beginning with third stitch from tip.
2 Knit all 3 stitches together, as if they were 1.
The result is a right-slanting double decrease.

3-NEEDLE BIND-OFF

Bind-off ridge on wrong side
1 With stitches on 2 needles, place ***right sides together***.
* Knit 2 stitches together (1 from front needle and 1 from back needle, as shown); repeat from * once more.

2 With left needle, pass first stitch on right needle over second stitch and off right needle.

3 Knit next 2 stitches together.
4 Repeat Steps 2 and 3, end by drawing yarn through last stitch.

Bind-off ridge on right side
Work as for ridge on wrong side, EXCEPT, with ***wrong sides together***.

BIND OFF IN PATTERN

As you work the bind-off row for fabrics other than stockinette and garter stitch, knit or purl the stitches as the pattern requires. The bind-off is more attractive and flexible than in all-knit.

WRAP & TURN (W&T)

Each short row adds 2 rows of knitting across a section of the work. Since the work is turned before completing a row, stitches must be wrapped at the turn to prevent holes. Wrap and turn as follows:

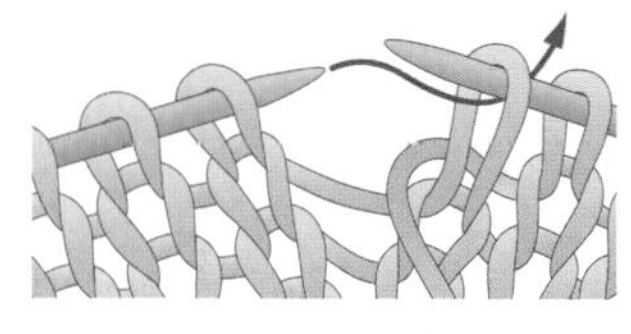

Knit side
1 With yarn in back, slip next stitch as if to purl. Bring yarn to front of work and slip stitch back to left needle (as shown). Turn work.
2 With yarn in front, slip next stitch as if to purl. Work to end.

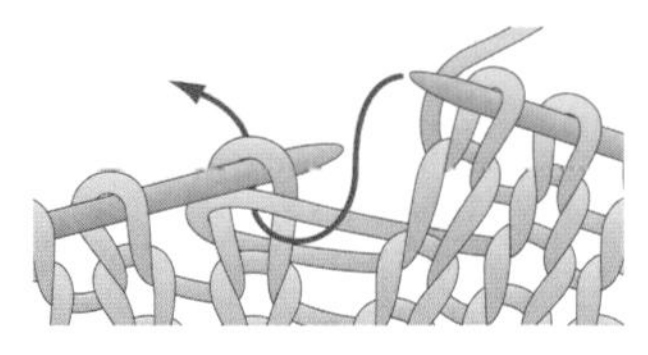

3 When you come to the wrap on a following knit row, hide the wrap by knitting it together with the stitch it wraps.

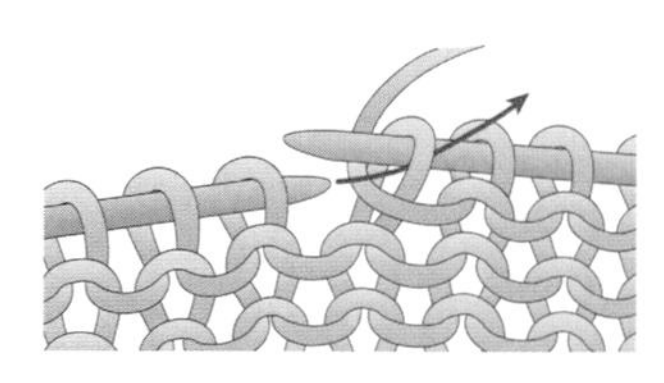

Purl side
1 With yarn in front, slip next stitch as if to purl. Bring yarn to back of work and slip stitch back to left needle (as shown). Turn work.
2 With yarn in back, slip next stitch as if to purl. Work to end.

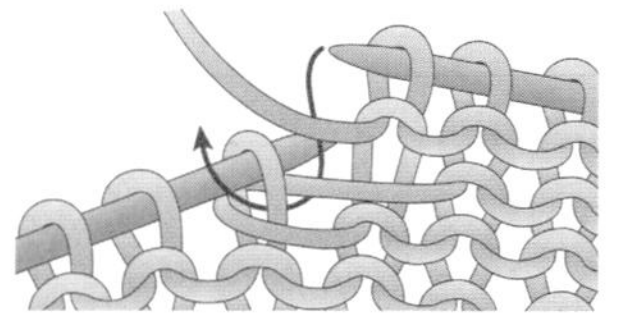

3 When you come to the wrap on a following purl row, hide the wrap by purling it together with the stitch it wraps.

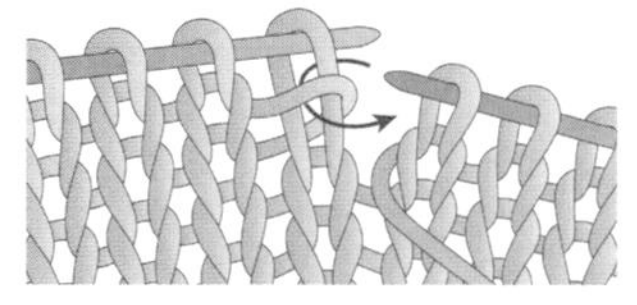

Purl a purl wrap
The first stitch of each short row is slipped (Step 2); this tapers the ends of short rows. When the wraps are hidden (Step 3), the mechanics of the shaping are almost invisible (see photo below).

KNIT THROUGH BACK LOOP (k1 tbl)

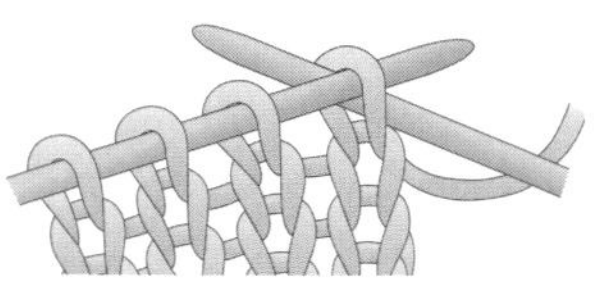

1 With right needle behind left needle and right leg of stitch, insert needle into stitch…

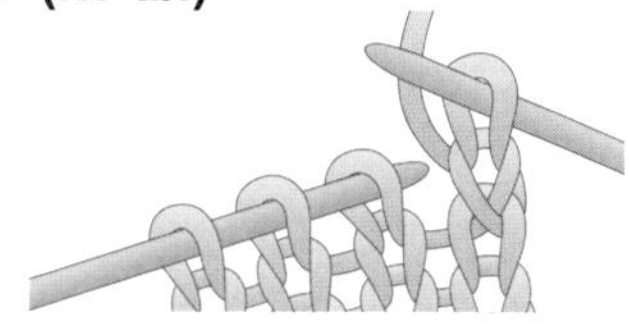

2 …and knit.

PURL THROUGH BACK LOOP (p1 tbl)

1 With right needle behind left needle, insert right needle into stitch from left to right…

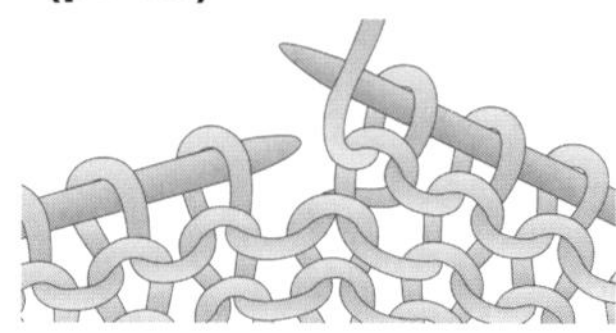

2 …and purl.

WORKING WITH 4 DOUBLE-POINTED NEEDLES (DPN)

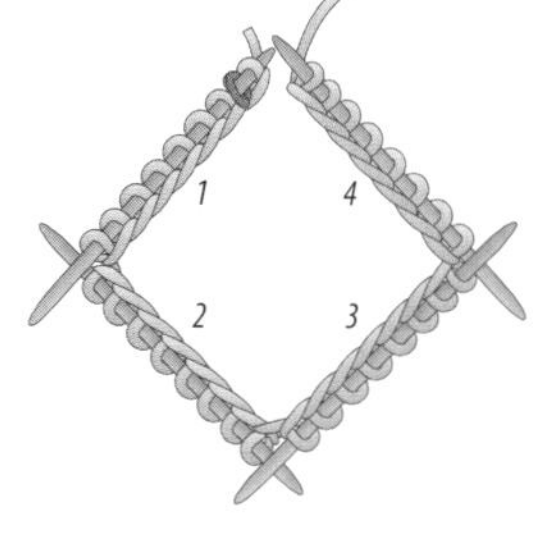

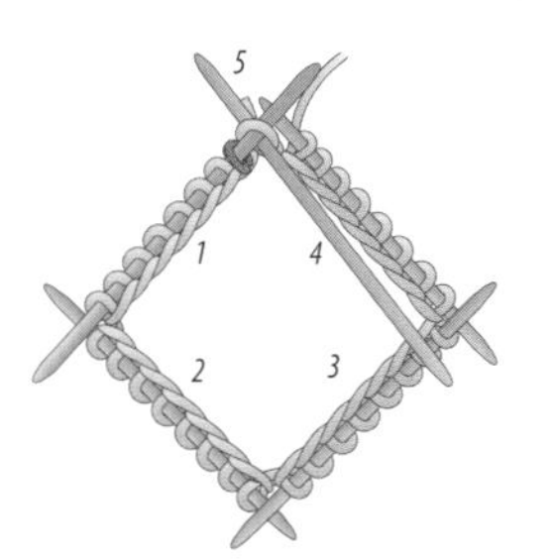

If instructions recommend working with a set of 5 dpn, arrange the stitches on 4 needles and knit with the fifth.
If instructions recommend working with a set of 4 dpn, arrange the stitches on 3 needles and knit with the fourth.

KNIT, PURL IN ROW BELOW (k1b, p1b)

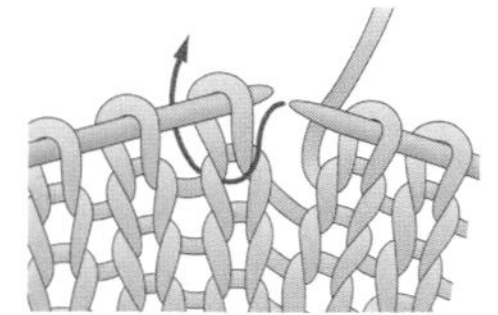

1 Instead of working into next stitch on left needle, work into stitch directly below it.

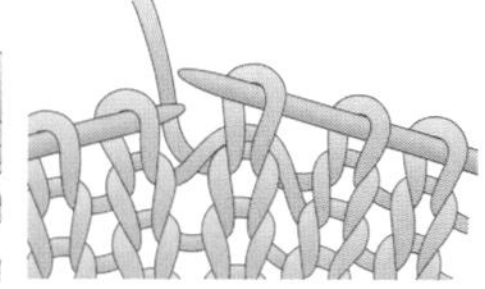

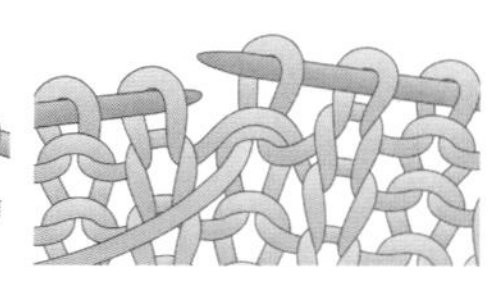

2 Pull stitch off left needle and let it drop.

INTARSIA - PICTURE KNITTING

Color worked in areas of stockinette fabric: each area is made with its own length of yarn. Twists made at each color change connect these areas.

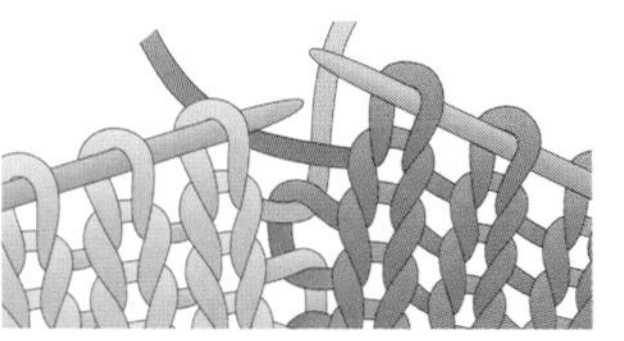

Right-side row

Wrong-side row

Making a twist:
Work across row to color change, pick up new color from under the old and work across to next color change.

4-TO-1 INCREASE AT OUTSIDE CORNERS

Work 4 half-double crochet stitches into the corner stitch, this rate of increase is repeated for each round.

3-TO-1 DECREASE

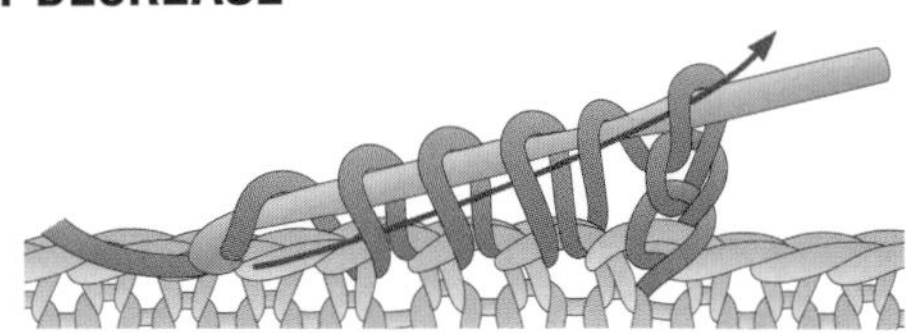

Yarn over, * insert hook into next stitch, catch yarn and pull through stitch only; repeat from * 2 times more—5 loops on hook. Catch yarn and pull through all 5 loops.

CHAIN STITCH EMBROIDERY

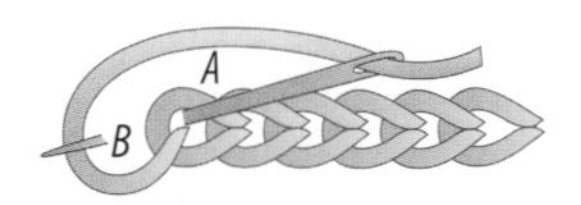

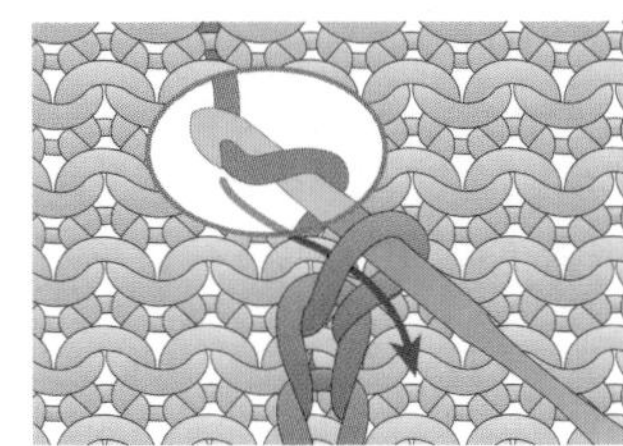

Chain stitch can be worked 2 ways:
1 Thread the yarn into a blunt needle, or …
2 … hold yarn on the wrong side of the fabric and a crochet hook on the right side.

BACKWARD SINGLE CROCHET, CRAB STITCH

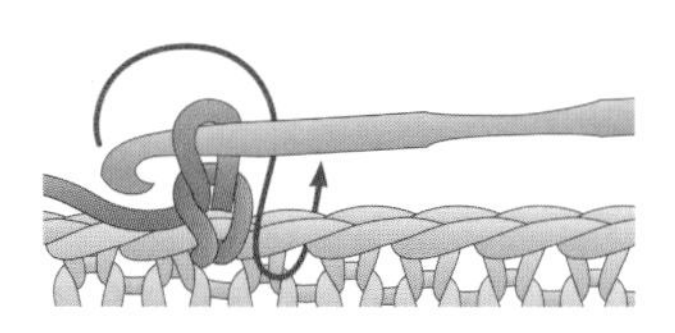

1 Insert hook into a stitch, catch yarn, and pull up a loop. Catch yarn and pull a loop through the loop on the hook.
2 Insert hook into next stitch to right.

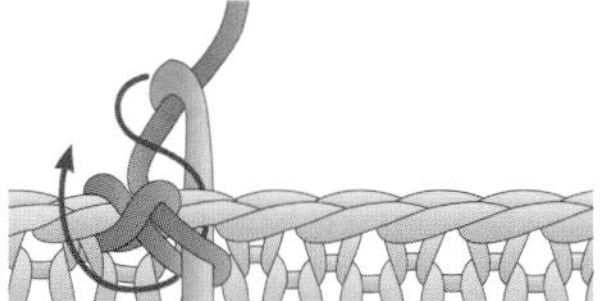

3 Catch yarn and pull through stitch only (as shown). As soon as hook clears the stitch, flip your wrist (and the hook). There are 2 loops on the hook, and the just-made loop is to the front of the hook (left of the old loop).

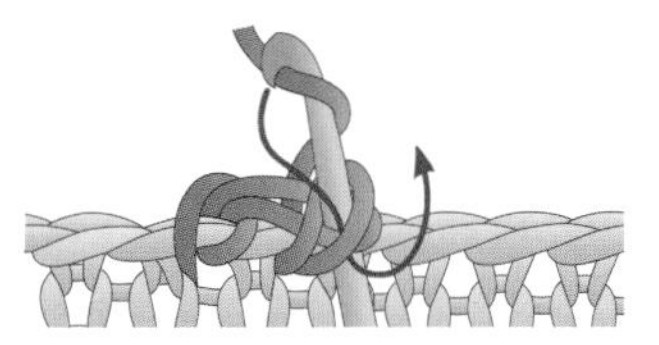

4 Catch yarn and pull through both loops on hook; 1 backward single crochet completed.

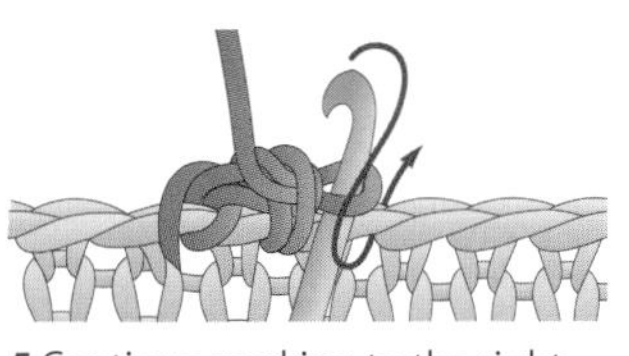

5 Continue working to the right, repeating Steps 2–4.

CHAIN STITCH (ch st, ch)

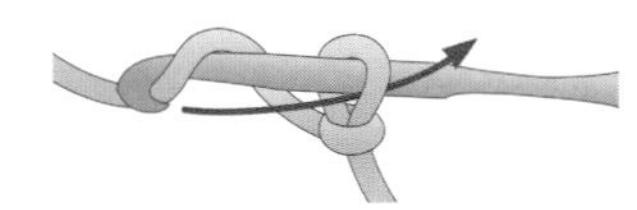

1 Make a slipknot to begin.
2 Catch yarn and draw through loop on hook.

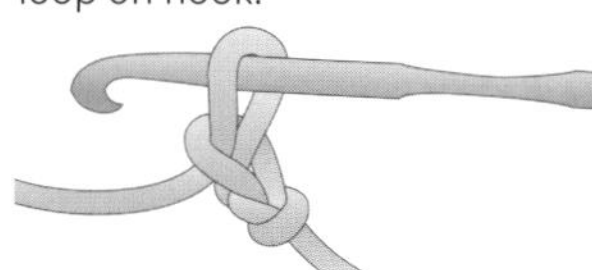

First chain made. Repeat Step 2.

HALF DOUBLE CROCHET (hdc)

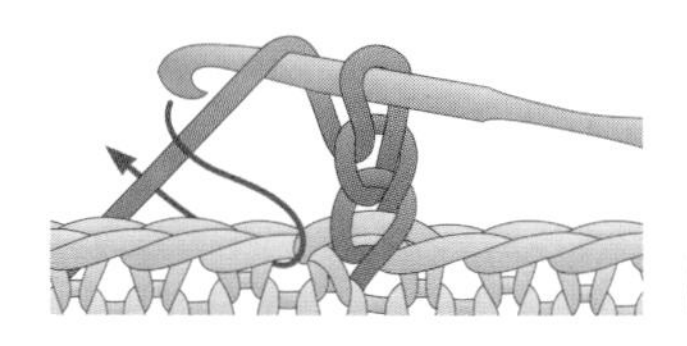

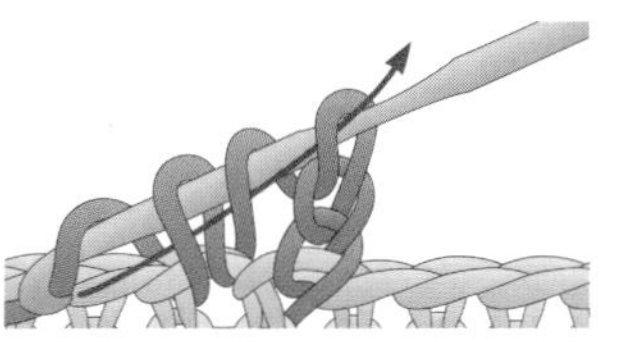

1 Insert hook into a stitch, catch yarn, and pull up a loop. Chain 2 (counts as first half double crochet).
2 Yarn over, insert hook into next stitch to the left (as shown). Catch yarn and pull through stitch only; 3 loops on hook.
3 Catch yarn and pull through all 3 loops on hook: 1 half double crochet complete. Repeat Steps 2–3.

DOUBLE CROCHET (dc)

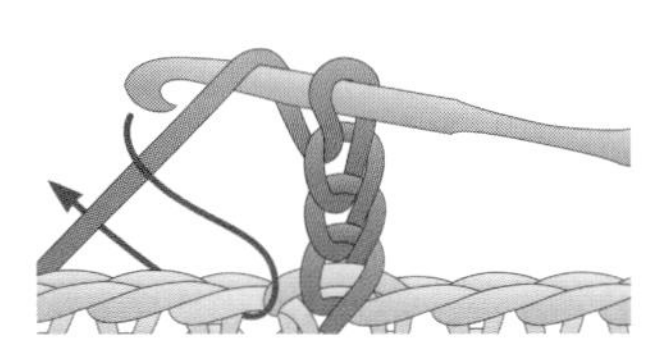

1 Insert hook into a stitch, catch yarn, and pull up a loop. Chain 3 (counts as first double crochet).
2 Yarn over, insert hook into next stitch to the left (as shown). Catch yarn and pull through stitch only; 3 loops on hook.

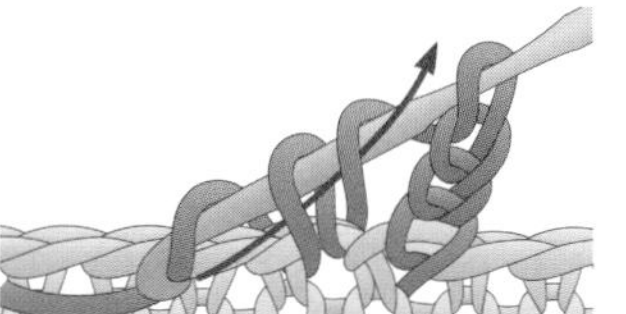

3 Catch yarn and pull through 2 loops on hook.

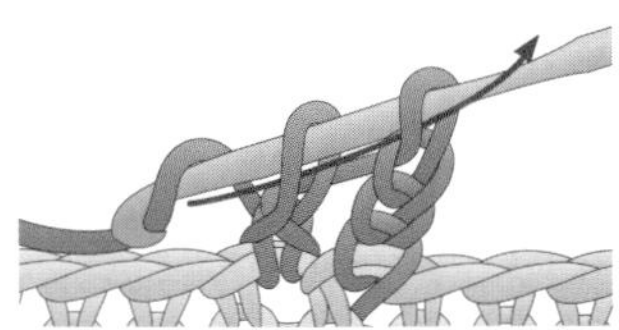

4 Catch yarn and pull through remaining 2 loops on hook. Repeat Steps 2–4.

SINGLE CROCHET (sc)

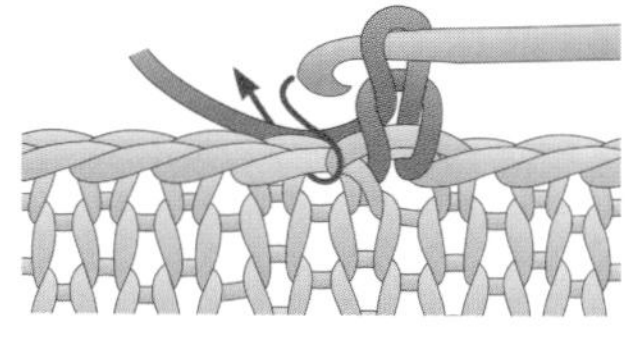

1 Insert hook into a stitch, catch yarn, and pull up a loop. Catch yarn and pull through the loop on the hook.
2 Insert hook into next stitch to the left.

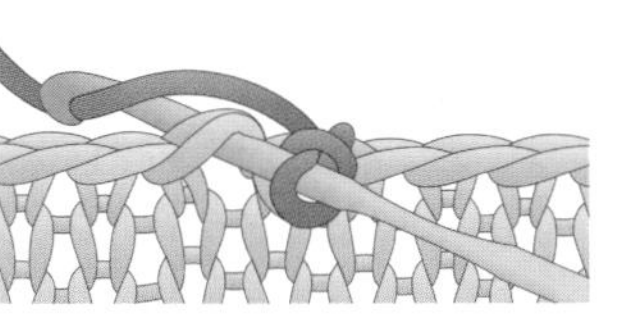

3 Catch yarn and pull through the stitch; 2 loops on hook.

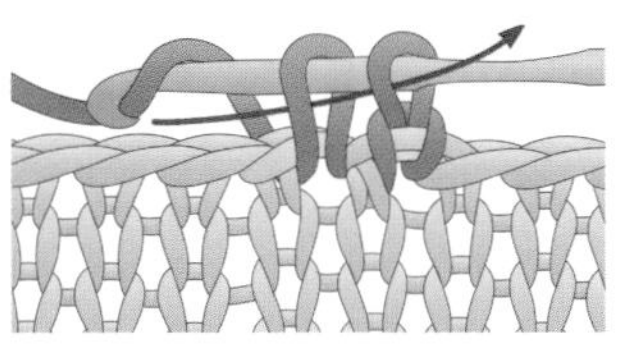

4 Catch yarn and pull through both loops on hook; 1 single crochet completed. Repeat Steps 2–4.

SLIP STITCH (sl st)

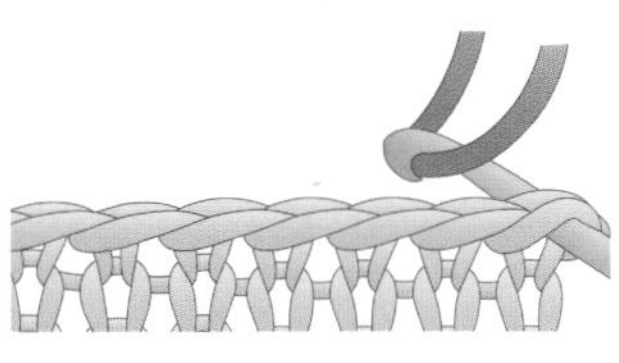

1 Insert the hook into a stitch, catch yarn, and pull up a loop.

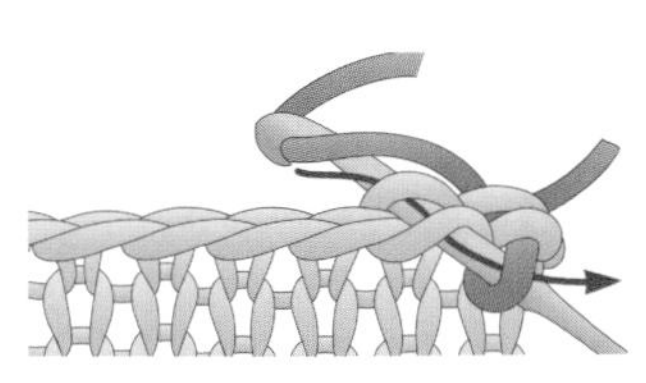

2 Insert hook into the next stitch to the left, catch yarn and pull through both the stitch and the loop on the hook; 1 loop on the hook. Repeat Step 2.

GRAFT IN STOCKINETTE

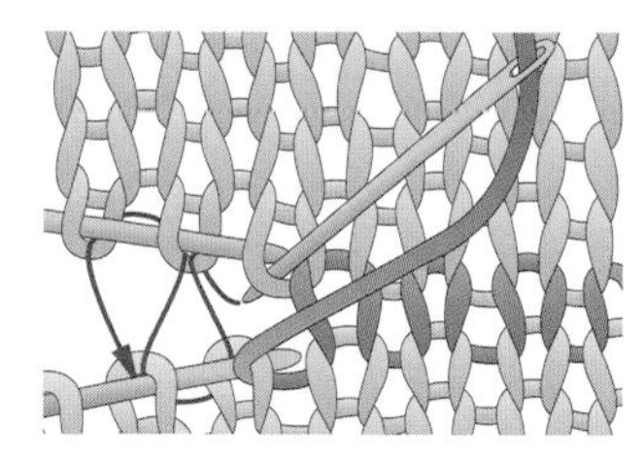

ON THE NEEDLES

1 Arrange stitches on 2 needles as shown.
2 Thread a blunt needle with matching yarn (approximately 1" per stitch).
3 Working from right to left, with right sides facing you, begin with Steps 3a and 3b:
3a Front needle: bring yarn through first stitch ***as if to purl,*** leave stitch ***on needle.***
3b Back needle: bring yarn through first stitch ***as if to knit,*** leave stitch ***on needle.***
4a Front needle: bring yarn through first stitch ***as if to knit, slip off*** needle; through next stitch ***as if to purl,*** leave stitch ***on needle.***
4b Back needle: bring yarn through first stitch ***as if to purl, slip off*** needle; through next stitch ***as if to knit,*** leave stitch ***on needle.***
Repeat Steps 4a and 4b until 1 stitch remains on each needle.
5a Front needle: bring yarn through stitch ***as if to knit,*** slip ***off needle.***
5b Back needle: bring yarn through stitch ***as if to purl,*** slip ***off needle.***
6 Adjust tension to match rest of knitting.

GRAFT IN GARTER

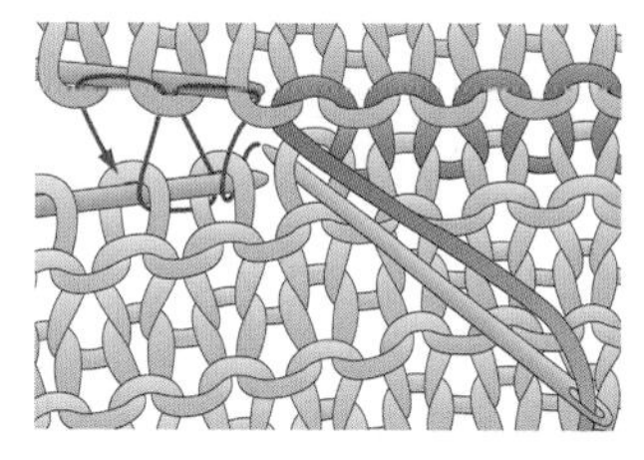

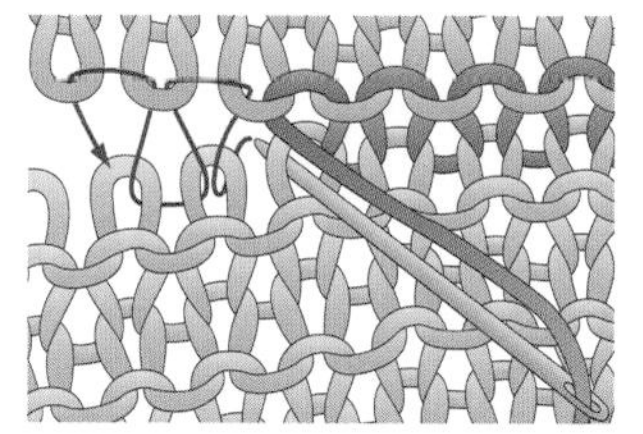

ON THE NEEDLES

1 Arrange stitches on 2 needles so stitches on lower, or front, needle come out of purl bumps and stitches on the upper, or back, needle come out of smooth knits.
2 Thread a blunt needle with matching yarn (approximately 1" per stitch).
3 Working from right to left, begin with Steps 3a and 3b:
3a Front needle: bring yarn through first stitch ***as if to purl,*** leave stitch ***on needle.***
3b Back needle: repeat Step 3a.
4a Front needle: bring yarn through first stitch ***as if to knit, slip off*** needle; through next stitch ***as if to purl, leave on*** needle.
4b Back needle: repeat Step 4a.
Repeat Steps 4a and 4b until 1 stitch remains on each needle.
5a Front needle: bring yarn through stitch ***as if to knit,*** slip ***off needle.***
5b Back needle: repeat Step 5a.
6 Adjust tension to match rest of knitting.

ATTACHED I-CORD EDGING

1 With dpn, cast on 3 or 4 sts, then pick up and k 1 st along edge of piece—4 or 5 sts.

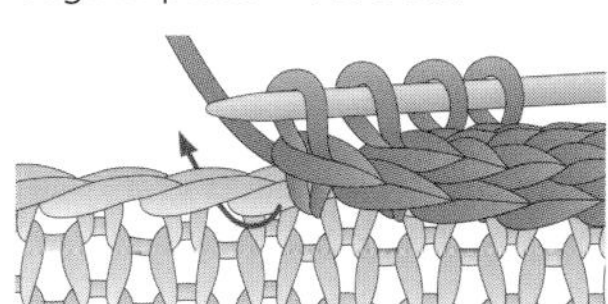

2 Slide sts to opposite end of dpn and k2 or k3, then k2tog through the back loops, pick up and k 1 st from edge. Repeat Step 2 for I-cord.

OVERCAST SEAMS

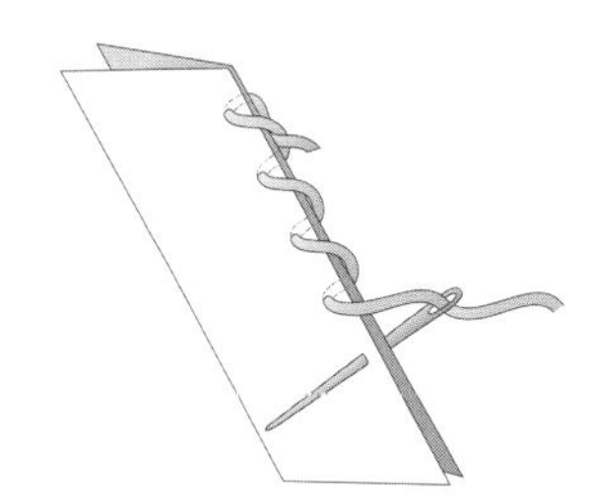

Overcast seams are perfect for quick seams. And work well for very textured yarns.

BACKSTITCH

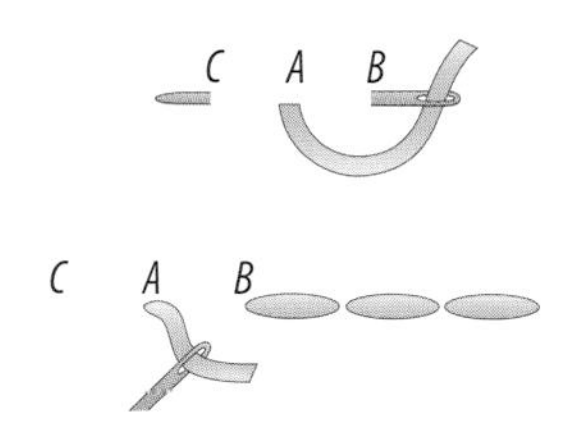

Bring needle out at A, down at B, and out again at C. Point C now becomes the point A of the next stitch.

MATTRESS STITCH

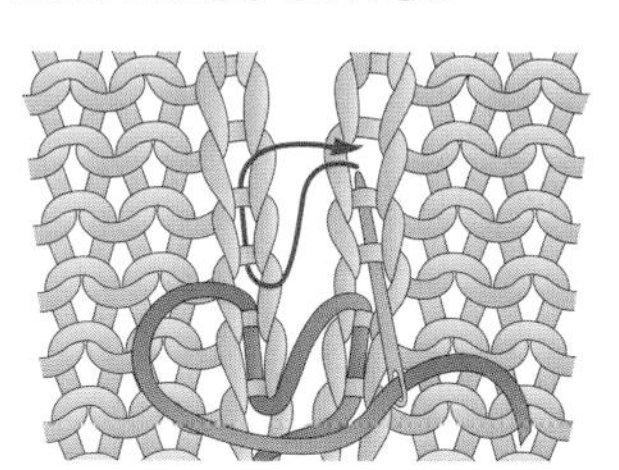

ATTACHING FRINGE

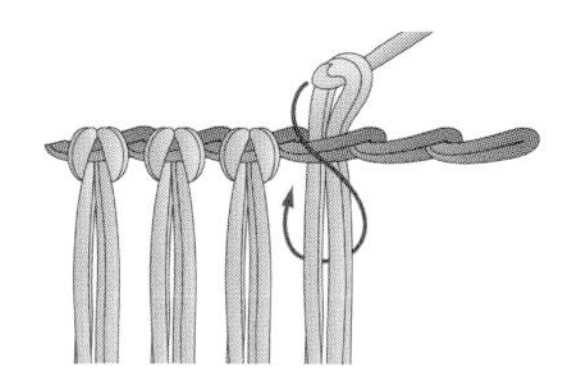

Cut lengths of yarn to twice desired length of fringe plus 1". Divide into groups of 2 or more strands.
1 Insert crochet hook from wrong side of work through a stitch at edge. Draw center of strands through, forming a loop.

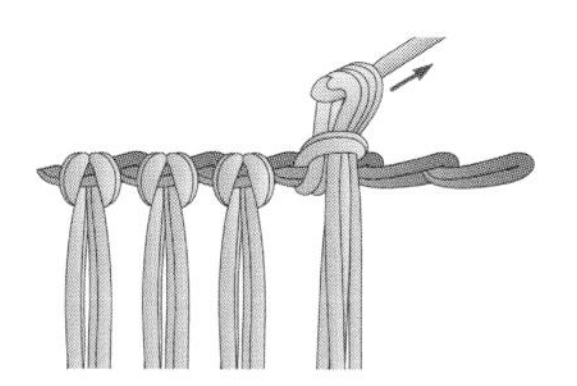

2 Draw ends through loop. One fringe section complete.

2-COLOR TWISTED CORD

1 Interlock strands of one color with strands of another color.
2 Tie knot at each end.
3 Twist tightly.
4 Fold in half and knot together.
5 Allow cords to twist together.

Beginner basics

KNIT CAST-ON

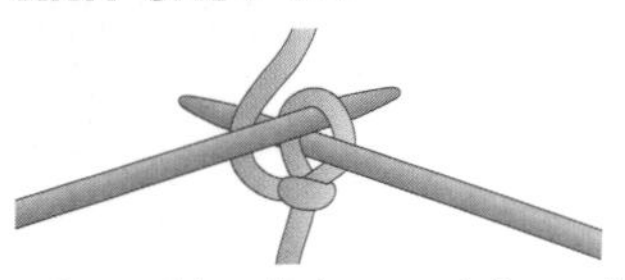

1 Start with a slipknot on left needle (first cast-on stitch). Insert right needle into slipknot from front. Wrap yarn over right needle as if to knit.

2 Bring yarn through slipknot, forming a loop on right needle.
3 Insert left needle under loop and slip loop off right needle. One additional stitch cast on.

4 Insert right needle into the last stitch on left needle as if to knit. Knit a stitch and transfer it to the left needle as in Step 3. Repeat Step 4 for each additional stitch.

KNIT

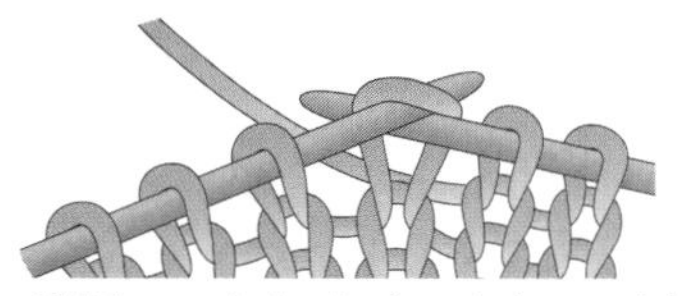

1 With yarn in back of work, insert right needle into stitch on left needle from front to back.

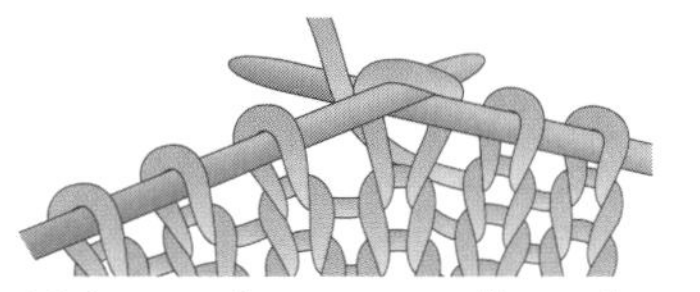

2 Bring yarn between needles and over right needle.

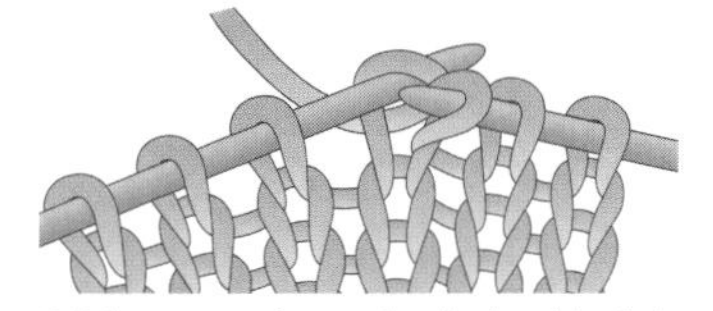

3 Bring yarn through stitch with right needle. Pull stitch off left needle.

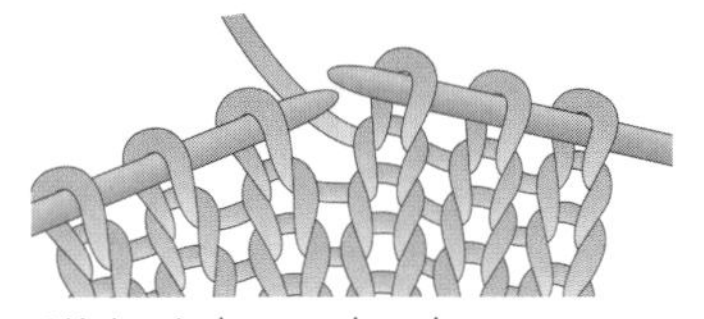

4 Knit stitch completed.

PURL

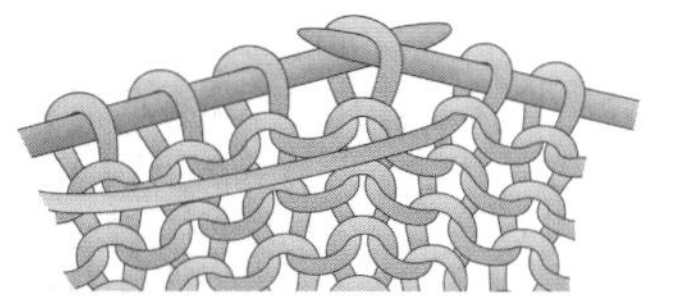

1 With yarn in front of work, insert right needle into stitch from back to front.

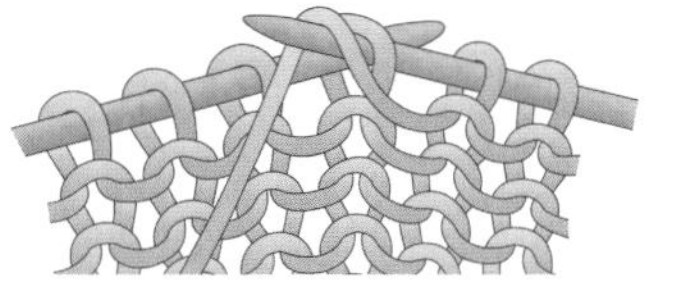

2 Bring yarn over right needle from front to back.

3 Bring yarn through stitch with right needle. Pull stitch off left needle. Repeat Steps 1–3.

BIND OFF KNITWISE

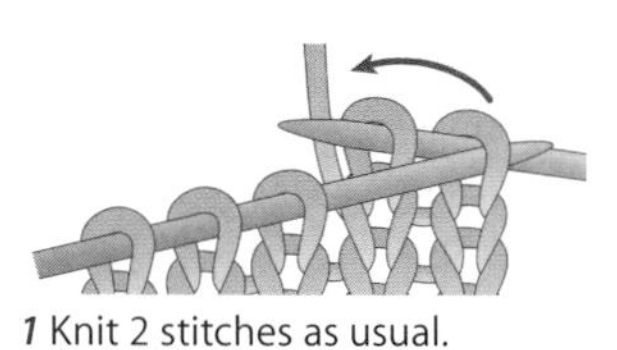

1 Knit 2 stitches as usual.
2 With left needle, pass first stitch on right needle over second stitch (above) and off needle: 1 stitch bound off (next drawing).

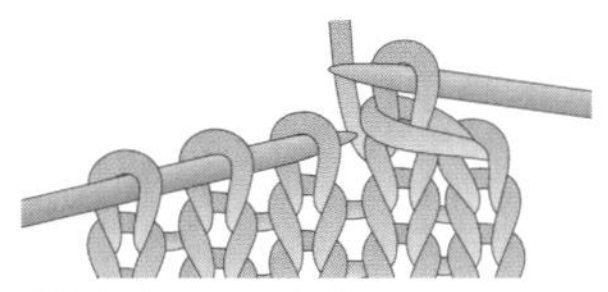

3 Knit 1 more stitch.
4 Pass first stitch over second.
Repeat Steps 3–4.
When last loop is on right needle, break yarn and pull tail of yarn through loop to fasten (see Fasten off).

BIND OFF PURLWISE

Work Steps 1–4 of Bind-off Knitwise except, purl the stitches instead of knitting them.

FASTEN OFF

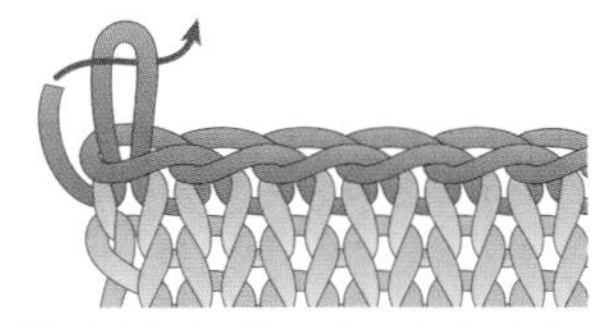

Work bind-off until only 1 stitch remains on right needle. If this is the last stitch of a row, cut yarn and fasten off stitch as shown above. Otherwise, this is the first stitch of the next section of knitting.

Working from charts

Charts are graphs or grids of squares that represent the right side of knitted fabric. They illustrate every stitch and the relationship between the rows of stitches.
Squares contain knitting symbols.
The key defines each symbol as an operation to make a stitch or stitches.
The pattern provides any special instructions for using the chart(s) or the key.
The numbers along the sides of charts indicate the rows. A number on the right side marks a right-side row that is worked leftward from the number. A number on the left marks a wrong-side row that is worked rightward. Since many stitches are worked differently on wrong-side rows, the key will indicate that. If the pattern is worked circularly, all rows are right-side rows and worked from right to left.
Bold lines within the graph represent repeats. These set off a group of stitches that are repeated across a row. You begin at the edge of a row or where the pattern indicates for the required size, work across to the second line, then repeat the stitches between the repeat lines as many times as directed, and finish the row.

Specs: At a glance

Use the charts and guides below to make educated decisions about yarn thickness, needle size, garment ease, and pattern options.

Yarn weight categories

Yarn Weight	1 Super Fine	2 Fine	3 Light	4 Medium	5 Bulky	6 Super Bulky
Also called	Sock Fingering Baby	Sport Baby	DK Light- Worsted	Worsted Afghan Aran	Chunky Craft Rug	Bulky Roving
Stockinette Stitch Gauge Range 10cm/4 inches	27 sts to 32 sts	23 sts to 26 sts	21 sts to 24 sts	16 sts to 20 sts	12 sts to 15 sts	6 sts to 11 sts
Recommended needle (metric)	2.25 mm to 3.25 mm	3.25 mm to 3.75 mm	3.75 mm to 4.5 mm	4.5 mm to 5.5 mm	5.5 mm to 8 mm	8 mm and larger
Recommended needle (US)	1 to 3	3 to 5	5 to 7	7 to 9	9 to 11	11 and larger

Throughout this book, the photo caption describes the yarns and colors in the photograph. If a yarn is not available, its yardage and content information will help in making a substitution. Locate the Yarn Weight and Stockinette Stitch Gauge Range ove 10cm to 4" on the chart. Compare the range with the information on the yarn label to fiind an appropritate yarn. These are guidelines only for commonly used gauges and needle sizes in specific yarn categories.

Needles/Hooks

US	MM	HOOK
0	2	A
1	2.25	B
2	2.75	C
3	3.25	D
4	3.5	E
5	3.75	F
6	4	G
7	4.5	7
8	5	H
9	5.5	I
10	6	J
10½	6.5	K
11	8	L
13	9	M
15	10	N
17	12.75	

Equivalent weights

oz		g
¾ oz	=	20 g
1 oz	=	28 g
1½ oz	=	40 g
1¾ oz	=	50 g
2 oz	=	60 g
3½ oz	=	100 g

Conversion chart

	X		=	
centimeters	X	0.394	=	inches
grams	X	0.035	=	ounces
inches	X	2.54	=	centimeters
ounces	X	28.6	=	grams
meters	X	1.1	=	yards
yards	X	.91	=	meters

Project Index

Afghans

Pillows

Sets

List of Contributors

Eugen Beugler
Traci Bunkers
Kathy Cheifetz
Lily Chin
Gerdine Crawford-Strong
Sandra Daignault
Susan Douglas
Edie Eckman
Dott Grubbs
Susan Levin
Paula Levy
Heather Lodinsky
Michele Maks
Elena Malo
Sue Mink
Laura Polley
Ann Regis
Gitta Schrade
Colleen Smitherman
Barbara Venishnick
Jill Wolcott
Diane Zangl